THE ESSEX HUNDRED

ESSEX HISTORY IN 100 POEMS with historical notes and timelines

compiled and edited by
Andrew Summers
and John Debenham

Illustrated by
Elizabeth Summers

www.essex100.com

Published by Summersbook (UK) Ltd
Cumberland House
24-28 Baxter Avenue
Southend –on- Sea
Essex SS2 6HZ

www.essex100.com

First published 2006
(Reprinted twice)
Second Edition March 2007
Third Edition June 2007
Compiled by Andrew Summers
and John Debenham
Illustrated by Elizabeth Summers

British library cataloguing in Publication Data
A catalogue record for this book is available from British Library
ISBN 9780955229503

Typeset and printed by 4 Edge Ltd
7a Eldon Way
Eldon Way Industrial Estate
Hockley Essex SS5 4AD

CONTENTS

Introduction

From the Romans - to Nuclear power - to the Space Shuttle. How and why has Essex played such a pivotal role in the development of British History? Some interesting facts and unusual events make up the remarkable history of Essex. In verse, in prose and illustration some of these facts are related and unusual events explained.

The Hundred

The 'Hundred' was the ancient system of land measurement dating from Saxon times. It was a subdivision of a county or shire and had its own court. It consisted of 100 hides or parcels of land, each capable of supporting a family, which could be an extended family of up to fifty people.

In 1085 William the Conqueror sent Royal Commissioners across the country to assess land and property holdings in order to settle continuous disputes over the collection of taxes. The result was the 'Domesday Book', a definitive account, which gave the county of Essex seventeen 'Hundreds' plus for good measure some 'Half Hundreds' too!

One of the oldest English counties, Essex derived its name from the sixth century Kingdom of the East Saxons. Its natural borders are the rivers Lea in the west, Stour in the north, Thames in the south and to the east the North Sea (formerly known as the German Sea or Ocean). The boundaries remained virtually unchanged for nearly 1500 years until local government reorganisation in 1965.

The Good and the Bad

The title of the book 'The Essex Hundred' is derived from our hundred poems that relate to specific events, places or people that have left their mark on the county. Starting with Boudica sacking Colchester in AD 60 through to Queen Elizabeth I rallying the troops in Tilbury at the time of the Spanish Armada, Essex has played a leading role in the development of British History. Turner's painting of 'The Fighting Temeraire' famously depicts British art at its best. Less well known is her Captain, who fought with Nelson at Trafalgar, Sir Eliab Harvey of Chingford. Captain Oates' heroic sacrifice in trying to save his colleagues on Scott's ill fated expedition has become legendary. He came from a family of explorers in the little known village of Gestingthorpe situated in the north of the county. Then Essex Boys were the heroes of England World Cup Triumph in 1966.

Of course not only heroes are included in the trawl through the county's history. There are the villains too. Lord Richard Rich, later Baron Rich, from Great Leighs came third in a BBC History poll of the worst Britons in history. Later, in the 1700s, Dick Turpin and his 'Essex Gang' created havoc in the Epping area, while the 'Coggeshall Gang' brought a reign of terror to mid Essex in the nineteenth century.

Timelines have been included to put each subject into a wider historical context and where possible present day locations and contact points are given.

Andrew Summers
John Debenham
Editors

Acknowledgements

Thanks are due to many people who have helped and encouraged us in bringing this book to publication. In particular we would like to thank Shirley Baker for her eagle-eyed reading, invaluable editorial suggestions and investigations in the far corners of the county. Thanks also go to Joanna Debenham for her diligent proof reading, Chris and David Harrison for their help in the conceptual stages, Ian Yearsley for his helpful advice and the members of Southend Poetry Society for ongoing inspiration and encouragement. We also thank Churchwarden Joyce McCarthy, for guiding us through the history of the Willingale Churches, and the Editor, 'Walden Weekly News' for permission to use 'The Writing on the Wall'. Research was made easier by the resources and helpful staffs of libraries throughout Essex, Essex County Records Office and Colchester and Braintree Museums.

A special thanks is due to Greg Debenham and Glenis Summers, who have provided support throughout, and made some incisive observations when they were most needed.

We are extremely grateful to Elizabeth Summers the artist who has produced a fantastic range of drawings that appear on the cover and throughout the book.

The book cover is based on the Ogilby and Morgan Map of Essex 1678 (ERO publication 24) and is reproduced courtesy of Essex Records Office.

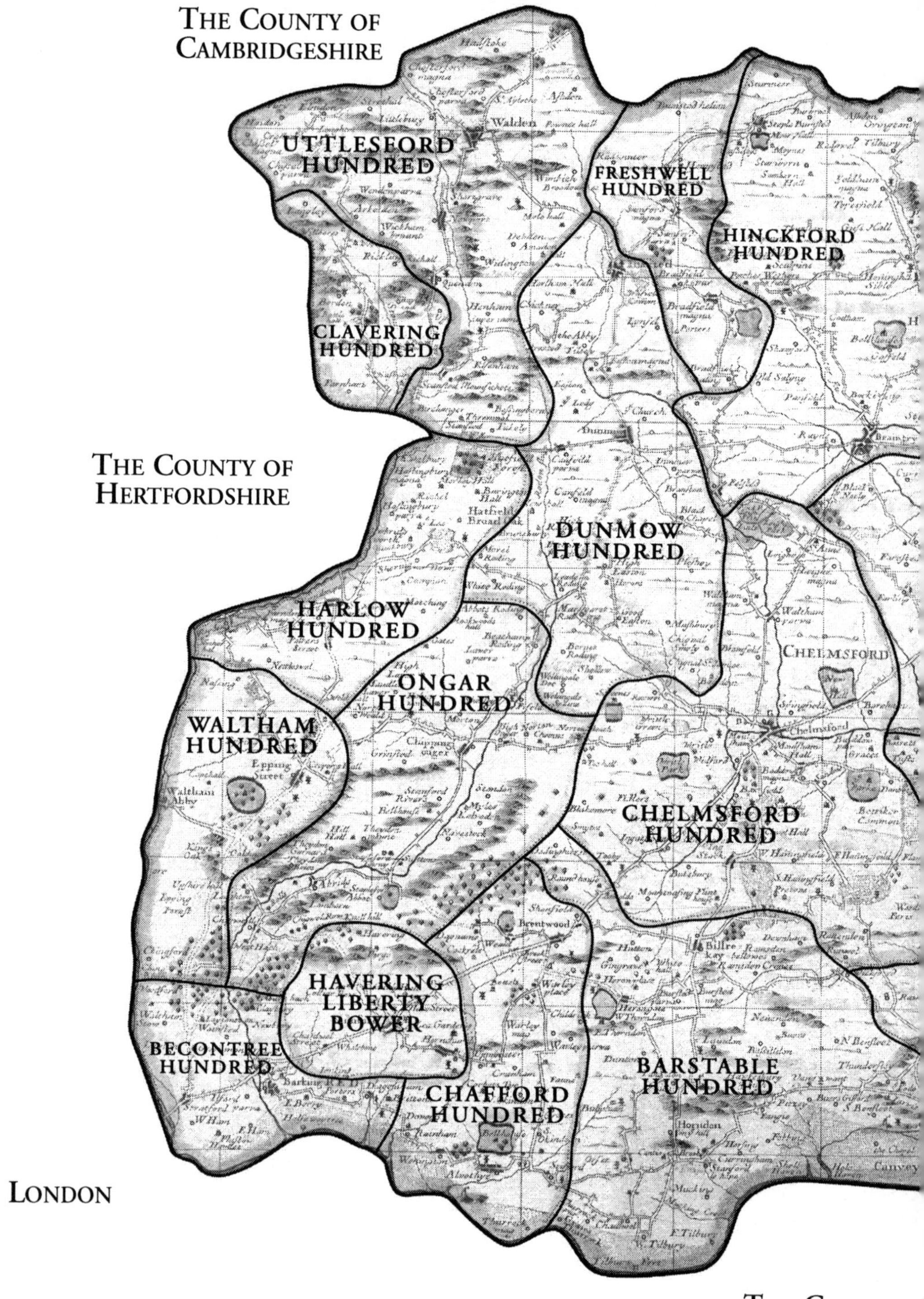
THE COUNTY OF CAMBRIDGESHIRE
UTTLESFORD HUNDRED
FRESHWELL HUNDRED
HINCKFORD HUNDRED
CLAVERING HUNDRED
THE COUNTY OF HERTFORDSHIRE
DUNMOW HUNDRED
HARLOW HUNDRED
ONGAR HUNDRED
CHELMSFORD
WALTHAM HUNDRED
CHELMSFORD HUNDRED
HAVERING LIBERTY BOWER
BECONTREE HUNDRED
BARSTABLE HUNDRED
CHAFFORD HUNDRED
LONDON
THE COUNTY
KENT

THE HUNDREDS OF ESSEX

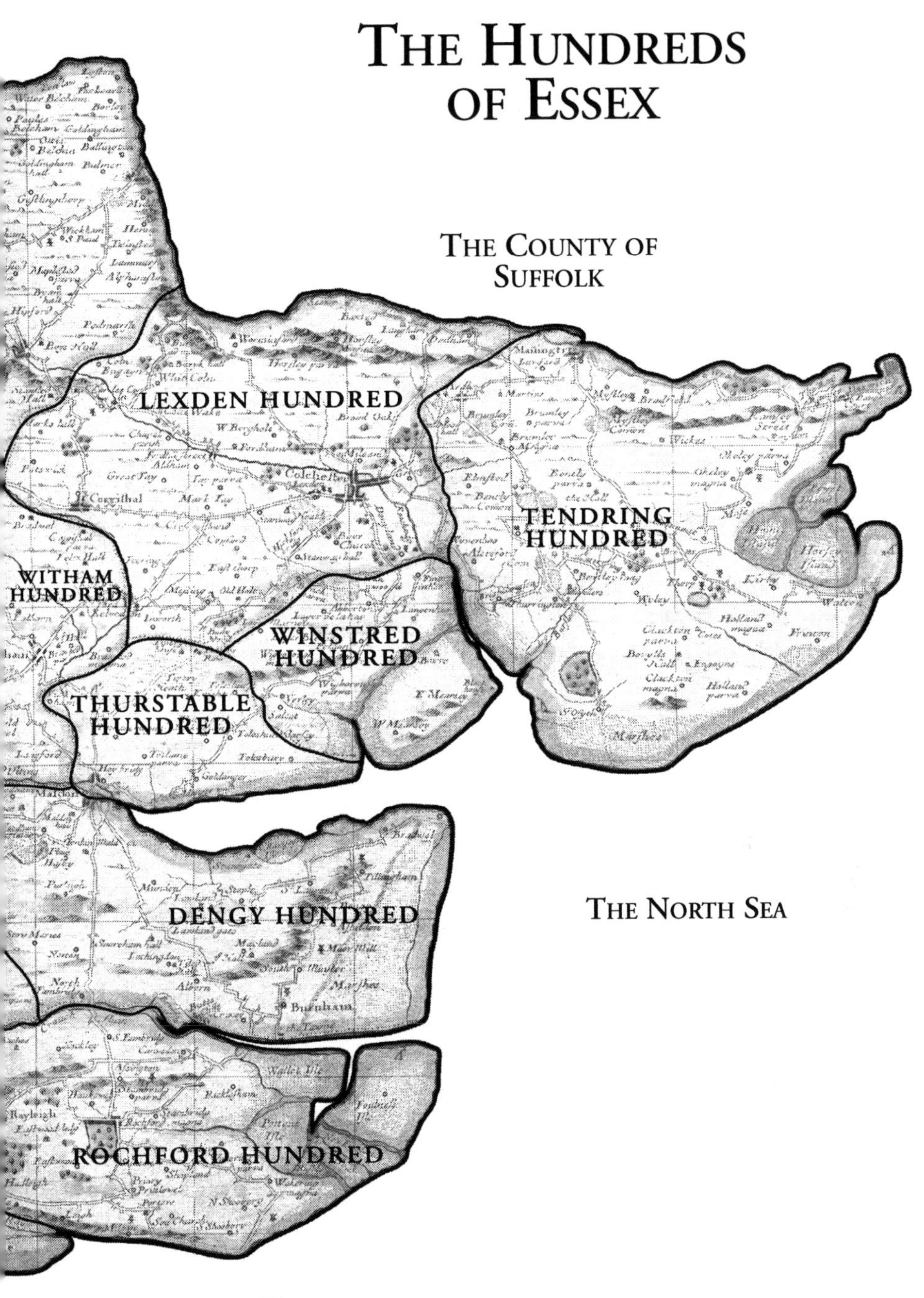

Timeline

Essex Event Commemorated	Date AD	National or International Event
	43	*Romans Invade England*
Boudica (Boadicea) sacks Colchester	60	*London designated capital of Britain*
Kingdom of the East Saxons founded	500	*St. David, Patron Saint of Wales born*
King Saebert buried in Prittlewell	630	*Mohammad captures Mecca*
St Cedd founds community at Othona	654	*Benedictines come to Peterborough*
Battle of Benfleet	893	*Bishop Asser writes 'Life of King Alfred'.*
Harold interred at Waltham Abbey	1066	*Battle of Hastings*
Sweyn's Castle built at Rayleigh	1070	*Hereward the Wake - Saxon Revolt*
Guernons become Monfichet	1071	*Norman invasion of Ireland,*
Robert de Vere oversees Magna Carta	1215	*Magna Carta signed at Runnymede*
Castle Hedingham falls to King John	1216	*King John succeeded by Henry III*
Hadleigh Castle started	1219	*Newgate Prison founded in London*
Edward III stays in Boxted	1354	*Birth of Owen Glendower*
Peasants revolt begins in Brentwood	1381	*Peasants revolt ends at Smithfield*
Death of John Hawkwood	1394	*Richard II goes to Ireland*
Duke of Gloucester seized at Pleshey	1396	*Gloucester murdered in Calais*
First recorded Pie Powder Court in Essex	1398	*Teutonic Order occupies Gotland.*
Richard Wright claims 'Dunmow Flitch'	1445	*Birth of Sandro Botticelli*
Edmund Tudor leaves Barking Abbey	1441	*Eton College founded.*
Henry Marney supports Henry Tudor for English Crown	1485	*Richard III dies at Bosworth Field* *Henry VII is first of Tudor dynasty*
Construction of Layer Marney Tower	1500	*First Caesarean birth in Switzerland*
Death of Lord Marney	1523	*Birth of Martín Cortés, conquistador*
Thomas Poyntz smuggles bibles	1536	*Willian Tyndale burnt at the stake*
Ann Boyleyn beheaded	1536	*Michaelangelo paints Sistine Chapel*
Leez Priory acquired by Lord Rich	1537	*Dissolution of Monasteries continues*
Hadleigh Castle sold to Lord Rich.	1552	*St Andrews Golf Club founded*
Richard Asser convicted at Maldon	1556	*Tobacco introduced to England*
'Baron' Rich founds Felsted School	1564	*Birth of William Shakespeare*
Harbingers inspect Mark Hall in Harlow	1576	*Martin Frobisher explores Canada*
Walden becomes Saffron Walden	1582	*William Shakespeare marries Anne Hathaway*
Queen Elizabeth I speaks in Tilbury	1588	*Spanish Armada defeated*
William Byrd moves to Stondon Massey	1589	*William Shakespeare writes - 'The Two Gentlemen of Verona'*

Boudica's monument on the river Thames opposite the House of Parliament in Westminster

Boudica's Revenge

With trumpeters and hornblowers
She came, shouting warcries
Armed with lance and shield
She charged in her chariot.

Swelling her neck
Gnashing her teeth
Brandishing her arms
The lioness roared.

For her husband's tribes
Her daughter's rape
She tracked the Romans down
Reducing the south to ash.

But the Watling Street Road
Slowed progress down
Entangled in the woods
The Iceni tribe died.

The great goddess of war
Remembered Cleopatra.
Better to drink potare
Than succumb to Rome.

Christine Billington

Historical Note: *Boudica (Boadicea) was Queen of the Iceni. With the Trinovantes from Essex she attacked Camulodunum Colonia (Colchester), a colony of retired Roman officers and their families in AD 60. Inside the city, the Roman defenders took refuge in the Temple of Claudius, but were overwhelmed and slaughtered. Colchester was then burnt to the ground.*
After sacking London and St Albans the British tribes were defeated by the Roman Governor Suetonius Paulinus in a pitched battle in the Midlands.

The King of Bling?

Christian King Saebba died and was interred,
In a simple wooden coffin he was laid to rest
With orthodox ceremony as his faith preferred,
His eyes with two golden crosses were blest.

His sons both Pagan had different ideas,
He should leave this world in style. Befitting
The traditions they had valued for years
Of a rich famous leader, and powerful king.

They built a chamber where his coffin was laid
Surrounding it with trappings of wealth
All manner of utensils and things were made
To ease his journey into the next life.

Now the things they gave their father as right
Are dug up, analysed, all written down.
But If the King had had his way then we might
Never have known of his love for our town.

His sons, Essex men of endeavour
Have made sure by doing their thing,
Their Dad's name will live for ever
As Southend and East Saxony's King of Bling!

John Debenham

***Historical note:** In 2004 a major excavation in Southend's Priory Park discovered the burial chamber of a Saxon king, probably Saebba. Possibly the most important Saxon find ever, throwing light on the little known 7th century in Essex.*

THE CHAPEL OF ST PETER-ON-THE-WALL

The Roman Fort of Othona guarded the Essex shore
On the Blackwater, near Bradwell-on-Sea.
When the Saxons arrived, Romans were no more
And their deserted Fort, just a pile of debris.

From the north came St Cedd, Christianity proclaiming,
To convert the East Saxons, and Sigbert their King.
From ruined Othona grew St Peter's-on-the-Wall
And St. Cedd its new Bishop, ministering to all.

Under the Normans the church of St Peter's
Passed to a French, Benedictine tradition.
Bought back for England 300 years later,
By Winchester's Bishop, William of Wykeham.

In the seventeen hundreds sadly the chapel
Had gone into rapid decline
For a long time it was used as a shelter for cattle
And as a barn for storing grain.

The 1920s brought the chapel's restoration,
With Christian services once more being read.
Providing shelter and an air of soulful reflection
And a lasting monument to the work of St Cedd.

John Debenham

Historical note: *In 654 St Cedd founded a community at Othona and built the Cathedral of St Peter on the Roman ruins. Regular services are held in the chapel of St Peters-on-the-Wall which, as its name implies stands close to the sea wall just south of Bradwell-on-Sea. In 1946 ex RAF chaplain, Norman Motley, founded the still thriving, Christian community of Othona a short walk from St Peters.*

St Peter-on-the-Wall

BENFLEET BATTLE HYMN
AD 893

Speak, ye chronicles of old,
Benfleet's story must be told.
From the shores of far-off time
Pluck the harp and sing this rhyme:

Sea-men blond and keen for plunder
Came to tear this land asunder.
Dragonships with force and stealth
Carried off the country's wealth.

Hardship followed where they passed.
England's hero came at last
From the bogs of Athelney,
Raised his standard strong and free.

To this young and shattered nation
Alfred was the inspiration.
Call on Thegn and Earl and Sax,
Blunt the pirates' bloody axe.

Men of will and warriors hoary
Took up arms for England's glory.
To pursue and halt and rout
Alfred sought the Vikings out.

Water sweet and harbour fair,
Benfleet was the sea-men's lair.
Hæsten Niger led the host,
Hero of the mead-halls' toast.

Over ditch and rampart thrust,
For revenge and glory lust.
Draw the anvil's heat-forged blades
And return the raiders' raids.

Danish shield meets Saxon spear
Send the fiends to flight in fear.
Soak the Downs with heathen blood.
Burn their ships on Benfleet's mud.

Hæsten, plundering abroad
Still escaped the Saxon sword.
Wife and hostages were taken
while he left his fort forsaken.

When the battle-din fell quiet
Odin wild and Thor retired.
Benfleet and its harbour-creek
Were blessed by Mary, virgin meek.

On that bloody, ancient spot
Rose a sacred house of God,
Claimed for all eternity
By peace and Christianity.

Robert Hallmann

Historical Note: *By A.D. 893 Alfred of Wessex, later Alfred the Great, had taken on the marauding hordes of Vikings. While he pursued one army to the west country, his son and son-in-law moved against those in the east who had established a camp at South Benfleet (beamfleote) under that infamous leader Haesten the Black. Together with reinforcements from London they surprised and stormed the Benfleet army, overpowered, killed and scattered them and burned or took away their ships. The wily Haesten was absent at the time.*

Not a lot of people know that!

Waltham Abbey a small market town
In Essex once belonged to The Crown.
Between Epping Forest and the River Lea in the west
As junction 26 on the M 25 it is now known best.

In Glastonbury a large flint cross was made
It was carried back to Essex in great cavalcade
Having mystical properties this Holy Rood
Was set in the church in a shrine to be viewed.

Of its healing powers many folk waxed lyrical,
They said touching the cross could work a miracle.
King Harold visited it and when he was cured
Of a paralysis, the church's future was assured.

Killed by that infamous arrow in the eye
Shot by a Norman at Hastings aiming high.
Six years after his death, it is said,
He was re-buried there in a coffin of lead.

Beside the present church building
An inscription, on a stone lying flat:
Reads; 'HAROLD KING OF ENGLAND 1066'
Now - 'Not a lot of people know that!'

Essex Man

Historical Note: *By the 1100s, the Waltham Abbey had become rich from the pilgrims flocking to the 'Shrine of the Holy Rood'. As part of his penance for the murder of Thomas à Beckett, Henry II re-founded the priory of Augustinian Canons in 1177, shortly after it was given Abbey status. Edward I and his wife, Eleanor, both lay in state at the Abbey for several weeks while their funerals were prepared in London. Henry VIII was another royal visitor. Henry caused the downfall of the Abbey when the monasteries were dissolved after the break with Rome. Waltham Abbey was the last to go in 1540 and it was then that the Holy Rood also disappeared.*

Sweyn's Castle

Your castle, Sweyn, is one of imagination,
A monument to a nation's invaders
Almost erased from the town.

The stones of your keep were taken
To rebuild the church, farmers
Have grazed their cattle on your ground

And now the site of your fortress
Is shadowed by a mill, whose sails are empty
Skeletons, restored only for show.

This is a measure of progress -
The feudal wars, the farm, and now a fantasy
Of which life relics may lay below.

Adrian Green

Historical Note: *Sweyn was one of the largest landowners in south Essex with Rayleigh his principal base. In 1070 he built a large earthwork castle on a high ridge with commanding views. This was recorded in the Doomsday survey of 1086;- 'et in hoc manerio fecit Suenue suum castellum'. (and in this manor Sweyn has made his castle) The castle changed ownership several times over the next 250 years, but eventually fell into decay and returned to farmland. The site is now managed by the National Trust.*

The Duke of Boulogne

Robert de Guernon fought with William the Conqueror
At the Battle of Hastings he won victory with honour.
A Cousin of the King, whose favour he gained,
As reward many English estates he obtained.

One of these was Stansted an Anglo-Saxon colony
It became his home, the headquarters of his Barony
Although he also held the Dukedom of Boulogne in France,
Now settled in Stansted he left nothing there to chance.

He built a motte and bailey castle; to rule from there his aim,
But he died and his son William changed the family name.
'Montfitchet' castle it would be, for now and ever after,
Until the last one, Richard, helped to force the Magna Carta.

With Richard de Montfitchet II, King John was quite annoyed
And in 1215, or thereabouts, Montfitchet castle he destroyed.
Richard was a brave knight and though the King his life did spare
With him the Montfitchet line ended, he died in 1258 with no heir.

Stansted had had Roman, Viking and Anglo-Saxon names
Then the Duke's family changed it to consolidate their claim.
Stansted became Montfitchet, from the Norman French derived
Then Anglicised to Mountfitchet, the name that has survived.

Art Szmauz

Historical Note: *After the Norman Conquest Robert de Guernon became the 15th Largest Landowner in England. Following the attack on the Castle around 1215 by King John, the stones were taken by the villagers to build houses. King John died the year following this attack and Henry III restored all the Montfitchet estates to Richard. Dying without heir, he never married, the estates were divided among his three sisters thus ending the Montfitchet line. The castle site lay overgrown and forgotten for 700 years until its re-construction in 1984 as a tourist attraction and is the only motte and bailey castle in the world. Next to the castle is the House on the Hill Toy Museum, which opened in 1991.*

MAGNA CARTA

June 15th 1215, at Runnymede King John made his seal
The Magna Carta was made law despite last minute appeal.
Robert De Vere, 3rd Earl of Oxford, was appointed to enforce
The Charter with 24 other Barons to ensure it ran its course.

De Vere, returned to Castle Hedingham, his ancestral seat,
To celebrate with a sumptuous banquet complete
With jousting and jugglers, and dancing laid on,
And toasts were drunk to the taming of King John.

The King, nominally complying with what he had signed,
On further examination found some clauses ill defined.
Far away Pope Innocent annulled the Magna Carta
Saying it was a conspiracy and just a fools charter.

The Magna Carta
Seal of 1215

King John retired to the countryside to plot a new tack
Within a year he had a plan to get his powers back.
He attacked and seized Rochester Castle without warning,
Then marched on de Vere at Hedingham next morning.

De Vere asked King Philippe's men to come to his aid
But the French, trapped at Colchester, were forcibly delayed.
King John's men laid siege, Castle Hedingham capitulated
De Vere's life was spared but his lands were confiscated.

Andrew Summers

Historical note: *The Magna Carta was a series of written promises between the King and his subjects. Of the 63 clauses many concerned England's legal system including, that laws should be good and fair and no freeman imprisoned or punished without going through the proper legal system. Shortly after the Hedingham Castle siege King John died in Newark having mysteriously lost the crown jewels whilst crossing the 'Wash' in East Anglia.*

Robert de Vere, 3rd Earl of Oxford was Lord Chamberlain of England and a crusader. He was one of the celebrated 25 barons appointed as Sureties to enforce the observance of the Magna Carta. On the death of King John, the new King Henry III made peace with the Barons, and Robert de Vere was returned to favour. Hedingham and all of his estates were returned. The de Vere Family flourished in Essex from the time of the Norman Conquest until the last Earl (20th) died in 1703.

HADLEIGH CASTLE

Hubert de Burgh laid the stone
With charter granted by the throne
Hadleigh Castle built on clay
Was Hubert's folly locals say?
T'will tumble down from its base
And like de Burgh fall from grace.

For 300 years the castle stood
Always needing to be made good
But King Edward tired of the expense
So ridded the castle as recompense.

Andrew Summers

Historical Note: *Hadleigh Castle was built for Hubert de Burgh in the early 13th century. Substantial additions were made in the 14th century by Edward III. It is these ruins that form the prominent estuary landmark visible today. The castle belonged to three of Henry VIIIs queens; Catherine of Aragon, Anne of Cleeves and Catherine Parr. In 1552 following the death of Henry VIII, his son Edward VI sold it to Richard Lord Rich for £700. Large parts of the castle were subsequently demolished and the stone removed for other building projects. In 1829 John Constable completed his painting of the Castle.*

Dog of War

In the north of the county on the banks of the Colne
Rests Heddingham castle and its village so named.
Where the son of a tanner left his mother to mourn
Sought the Black Prince of England, with passion to tame.

His resolve was soon tempered in bloodshed and thunder
'Til in battle at Crecy our blade won his spurs,
Trusted knight to a King, loyal man to his cause
Ink still wet on the treaty...the army dispersed...

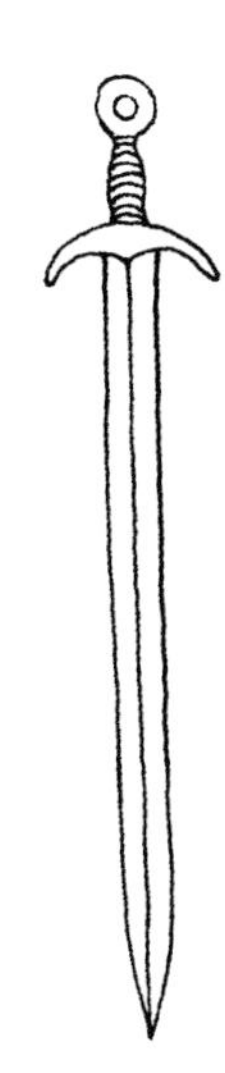

Now a soldier of fortune, his cause was his own
With a mercenary band, 'dogs of war' to a man,
His adventure now lay with the feuds of the south
And this bold restless warrior rode out for Milan.

For the sword skills he offered, the Milanese paid
As did Naples, Verona, 'Save us from the North!'
And so Hawkwood continued his dangerous venture
Condottieri! They hailed, 'English hero go forth...!'

And with every campaign came new glory and fortune
For the purse of the Pope was both generous and full
General, Soldier, Tactician he passed into legend
John Hawkwood brought justice to 'Lords of Misrule'.

'Til the years slowed his bloodlust and marriage his wanderings
And his death prompted all of acquaintance to weep
Though in Florentine splendour exalted in marble
Sible Hedingham church is the place where he sleeps.

Karen Bowman

Historical Note: *"Sir" John Hawkwood, was perhaps the original Soldier of Fortune. Born in 1320 in Essex, John Hawkwood learnt his craft under Edward III at the Battle of Poitiers in 1356. Later he plied his trade in Italy as a condottiere, (mercenary general) serving the highest bidder and even fighting under the Papal banner. Known locally as Giovanni Acuto he died in 1394. His remains were transferred to Sible Hedingham for burial. There is a commemorative fresco by Paolo Ucello in the Duomo in Florence.*

One Night in Boxted

Peter de Boxtede was much favoured by royalty.
Made Sheriff of Essex as reward for his loyalty.
From home the King's business took him away
To raise taxes and deal with those unwilling to pay.

While Sybil de Boxtede left alone in Boxted Hall
Made things nice and cosy while waiting nightfall
Bathed, perfumed, dressed in her finest lace
She brushed her hair and made up her face.

King Edward III had come to nearby Colchester's estate
And official records show he entered by the Balkerne gate.
Yet he left almost immediately so what was going on?
Local dignitaries waited patiently, but the king had gone.

At dusk a party of riders in Boxted appeared.
One had his face hidden, was he to be feared?
He strode to the halls door and embraced Sybil tight
The door closed behind him as dusk turned to night.

With the dawn this man, stepping sprightly emerged
His bodyguards all ready immediately converged.
Then they were gone. Sybil composed herself and waited.
Peter would be home soon. This was the part she hated.

Essex Man

Historical note: *Edward III visited Colchester in 1354. He was aged 41 at the time and married to Philippa of Hainault. During Edward's reign 'Treason' was defined by statute for the first time (1352) and English replaced French as the national language (1362). Peter de Boxtede died shortly afterwards and Sybil remarried. Their son also called Peter left England with John of Gaunt, the King's third son to fight in the Spanish Wars. In 1441 Richard de Boxtede, Peter senior's grandson became bankrupt and was forced to sell Boxted Hall.*

KING EDWARD III 1354

Three days that shook the Kingdom
Brentwood

Thomas Brampton, King Richard's Tax collector
Empowered to deal harshly with any objector.
Entered Brentwood with his clerks in tow,
Any waiver requests would be met with firm NO!

At Thomas á Becket's Chapel on the last day of May
He was greeted by Essex folk wanting their say,
Their leader was one Thomas Baker of Fobbing,
Chanting "We won't pay, you stop your robbing!"

The rabble grew louder roaring support,
Terrifying Brampton and his little court.
"Retreat," said Thomas, "the King will understand,
He'll know how to deal with this mutinous band"

Three days later in splendour into town rode
A Chief Justice no less, to impose the tax code.
Judge Robert Belknap his officials at his side
Was determined to collect and not be defied.

Confronting the crowd he made himself heard,
"I've come for what is owed and that's my last word."
The rabble's mood darkened as the Judge cried,
"Seize that man, the leader, as a rebel he'll be tried."

The 5,000 strong mob were inflamed by this retort
And promptly set upon both the judge and his court.
Stripped of his fine robes, his baggage set alight,
The judge though humiliated escaped and took flight.

His men were beheaded satisfying the mob's lust
Heads put on spikes, bodies dragged in the dust.
The peasants made their point in the bloodiest way
Then set off for London on their rebellious foray.

Art Szmauz

Historical Note: *The Peasant's Revolt or Great Revolt began in Brentwood, Essex on 31st May 1381. It had been sparked by what was considered an unfair imposition of tax on the poorer members of society. The Essex Rebels joined with those of Kent led by Wat Tyler, laid siege to London and nearly toppled the government. Two weeks later, on 15th June, Wat Tyler confronting Richard II at Smithfield, was killed after a skirmish with William Walworth the mayor of London. The Revolt was effectively over. Most of the other rebel leaders were hunted down and executed. Richard II was 14 at the time. Wat Tyler is remembered today as a hero of the people and commemorated in Pitsea by the 'Wat Tyler Country Park'.*

RETRIBUTION

Essex was where 'The whole madness first sprang'
So it was only natural the ringleaders would hang.
The King lodged in Writtle where his edicts flowed
For seven days, in a torrent that never slowed.

In Chelmsford's tollhouse the court was in session
Demanding from the rebels a sworn confession.
Justice was swift with no appeal, no mercy shown.
All pleas were rejected; the rebel leaders sent down.

The King withdrew promises he'd earlier made
Saying they were only granted when he was afraid
"I cannot uphold guarantees given under duress
Heed what I say carefully and hear what I stress."

"'Villeins ye are still and villeins ye shall remain."
There was no doubt King Richard spoke plain.
Decisively from strength he now laid down the law,
The rebellious peasants had rocked him to the core.

Andrew Summers

Historical Note: *After the peasants revolt had been suppressed King Richard II moved to Chelmsford and lodged in his manor house at Writtle from 1st July until 6th July 1381. For seven day it was the seat of Government. Over 145 rebel leaders were identified. Many escaped, but those apprehended were executed after a short trial, with all their properties confiscated. Parliament declared a general amnesty on 14 December 1381. The word Villien is derived from the French or Latin villanus, meaning serf or peasant, someone who is tied to the land and manor.*

The Silence of Pleshey Castle

Shakespeare remembered that sad sad place
That lies amidst its village, chained and locked
Of its hustle and bustle remains not a trace,
As if cursed and shunned and by hist'ry forgot.

The bailey lies empty, the bald motte stands bare.
The ancient brick bridge spans the moat quite forlorn.
You'll find no stockade, no proud tower there
From the home of the Gloucesters' the heart has been torn.

But once here were hunts and fine ladies and knights,
A chapel, bright gardens and bowers of scent,
Milady Eleanor enjoyed the delights
With her husband Thomas of royal descent.

Her husband the Duke and his brother, at pains
Had ruled the land when the King was a child,
Brought honour to England in foreign campaigns,
But old habits - and intrigue - die hard and stay wild...

For the King was of age now and proving his worth
Saw his uncle as a thorn to excise.
In 1397 Richard tracked him to earth
To Pleshey, while plotting his uncle's demise.

Persuaded old Gloucester to follow his train
Back to London, to honour and glory -
Transported instead to Calais and slain
Out of sight, in a deed foul and hoary.

Robert Hallmann

Historical Note: *Pleshey castle dates from the Norman era. It was acquired through marriage by Thomas of Woodstock, later the Duke of Gloucester and also the youngest son of Edward III. Gloucester was King Richard II's uncle. Disillusioned with the King's stewardship of the country he managed with the other 'Lord Appellants' to seize power. Richard II later regained power and eliminated his enemies one by one. In September 1397 Gloucester was tricked into leaving Pleshey for London. At Stratford he was ambushed, then transported to Calais in France where he died a few days later under mysterious circumstances. Pleshey Castle's claim to fame stems from its mention in Shakespeare's play "Richard II," where the author blames the King for Gloucester's death.*

Sanctuary at Barking

Henry V died leaving widow Catherine
And baby son Henry to reign as king.
Owen Tudor then made Catherine his wife,
Of lowly rank he was the love of her life.

They had four children 'ere their secret was known.
Children were one thing but marriage quite another.
The governing council in turmoil was thrown,
This would not do for the young King's Mother.

Owen fled to Wales, Catherine to Kent.
Their children to Barking Abbey were sent,
To be cared for said Henry, their half-brother,
By the Abbess acting as surrogate mother.

Jasper next became Pembrokeshire's Earl,
While Edmund married the Beaufort girl,
Margaret, a match made in heaven -
They had a son Henry - King number seven?

Henry eventually laid claim to the crown,
The bloodshed and turmoil of battle died down,
With the wars of the roses over and done.
Peace for a while; Tudor reign had begun.

John Debenham

Historical Note: *The AD 666 Barking Abbey of St Erkenwald was destroyed by the Vikings in 870. Rebuilt as a Benedictine Royal Foundation in the tenth century, William the Conqueror is known to have spent his first New Year in England staying there in 1066. Among the Abbesses were numbered Queens, Princesses and members of the nobility. Katherine de la Pole, sister of the Earl of Suffolk, was the Abbess that took care of the Tudor children, probably at the behest of their half-brother king Henry VI. Today only the ruins of the Abbey remain. A short distance from the town centre these are open to the public at all times.*

Curfew Tower Barking Abbey

The Dunmow Flitch

'You shall swear by the Custom of our Confession
That you never made any Nuptial Transgression'

In 1104, two lovers came
And knelt before the Holy Prior;
They wanted to prove that it was true
You could be married and in love too.

The Prior gave them a Bacon Flitch
Then they revealed they were very rich
And gave to him some precious land
So you see, they had this planned.

More couples arrived every year
Kneeling on pointed stones to declare
That they too were wed and in harmony
Deserving of Bacon and a ride in the Chair.

The tale of the flitch became well known
As Chaucer recalled in 'The Wife of Bath'
Little Dunmow danced with glee at the fame
As they carried the winners down the Church path.

Since Great Dunmow took over the flitch
Queen Elizabeth II was awarded the prize
Her golden wedding she celebrated
And seventeen local couples were fêted.

'For this is our Custom at Dunmow well known
Though the sport be ours, the bacon's your own.'

Shirley Baker

***Historical Note:** The Dunmow Flitch, dates from 1104 when, a year and a day after their marriage, Reginald Fitzwalter and his wife, dressed humbly and begged blessing of the Augustinian Prior of Little Dunmow. Impressed by their devotion, the Prior bestowed upon them a Flitch of Bacon. Revealing his identity as Lord of the Manor, Fitzwalter gave his land to the Priory on the condition a Flitch should be awarded annually to any couple who could claim similar devotion. The earliest recorded successful claimant is Richard Wright in 1445, although it is mentioned earlier by Chaucer in 'The Wife of Bath's Tale'. Now held in Great Dunmow every leap year the town still rewards the successful claimants with a side, or flitch, of bacon and being carried in the ceremonial chair to the Market Place.*

Just Mad About Saffron

As far as the eye could see saffron grew,
Shining purple and white in the morning dew,
In every Monastery garden and available field
The Abbot anticipated a bumper yield.

An Arabian plant, at most a foot high,
Harvested for medicine, cooking or dye.
The flower's orange heart provided the source
Of this commodity haggled for with such force.

Each flower's three stigmas plucked by hand in a trice,
75,000 flowers produced but one pound of the spice.
Nimble fingers were needed so valuable was the crop.
The Abbot waited for his tithe: a tenth off the top.

Local wool dyed with Saffron brought wealth and fame
The economy boosted, the town again changed its name.
To the Saxon 'Walden' adding 'Chipping' had caused no fuss
So it was renamed 'Saffron Walden' to honour 'Crocus Sativus.'

Art Szmauz

Historical Note: *The spice Saffron is taken from the stigma of the saffron crocus, Crocus Sativus. It was a highly prized commodity from the 12 century onwards, buyers would travel great distance to acquire it. Wool was major product in England, and Essex especially, and the demand for saffron dye was high until the collapse of the wool trade in the 18th century. Introduced in the14th century into what was then Cheyping, later Chipping, Walden the town became a major supplier of Saffron. The spice contributed to centuries of prosperity. It was to honour this that the name was changed to Saffron Walden in the mid 16th century. It was the only town in England to be associated with the precious crop in this way.*

Loyal Subject
Henry Marney

On Bosworth's bloody field Henry Marney made his name.
Richard III had lost the crown to which Henry VII now laid claim.
The Wars of Roses were over and the new King on the throne
Rewarded the loyalty of his friends, and Marney came into his own.

Appointed to the Privy Council ever close to the new King's side,
As a Knight of the Bath he was to Henry, both confidante and guide.
Promoted to Captain of the Guard Marney faithfully served the nation
And was ennobled, by his old friend's son, at Henry VIIIs coronation.

Marney built himself a home, which he thought
Magnificent enough for his standing at court.
Layer Marney Tower now stands serenely on its perch
A landmark for miles close by St Mary's church.

John Debenham

Historical Note: *Layer Marney Tower was built in the early 1500s. The tower is 80ft (25m) high. Lord Marney had intended to extend and build it in similar style to that of Hampton court. Lord Marney died in 1523. His son John inherited but died two years later leaving no heir to continue the construction. The estate passed to Sir Brian Tuke whose family, in 1579, were host to a visit by Queen Elizabeth the First. (She is believed to have slept in what is now the billiard room.)*

To Marry a King

The thwack! of golf balls on the green
At Rochford 100 golf course, so serene.
Rochford Hall was also once home to Thomas Boleyn
And his daughter Anne who grew up to be Queen.

A family man, with two daughters and a son,
Boleyn was keen for all his children to get on.
Mary his eldest was groomed for the court
And quickly became Henry's favourite consort.

Mary gave in too easily to the King's desires
Then when he met Anne, was promptly retired.
But sister Anne was made of sterner stuff
For her only marriage was good enough.

Henry changed the rules; divorced Catherine his wife,
Took Anne as his queen and found a new lease of life.
She bore him a daughter a future Queen Elizabeth:
Producing daughters, not sons, would lead to her death.

Though rumours circulated that Queen Anne played around,
With brother George amongst others, no proof was found.
Jane Seymour was spotted. Henry ordered Anne's demise.
To the block she went with George. Both convicted by lies.

And what of Mary? She'd escaped the King
Whatever it was for her, for him it was just a fling.
She went home to Rochford, avoiding the fate
Of both Anne and George, and inherited the estate.

John Debenham

Historical Note: *In 1525 Thomas Boleyn was made Viscount of Rochford. His daughter Anne who would become Queen and mother of Elizabeth I, was courted by Henry VIII at Rochford Hall, they married in 1533. Anne's failure to produce a male heir, her many enemies at court and the King's roving eye, all combined to her being tried on charges of treason and adultery, and beheaded in 1536. Within one month of the execution Henry married Jane Seymour. Mary died in 1542, the last of the Boleyn family in England. Rochford Hall is now partly residential and also forms part of Rochford Hundred Golf Club.*

Tyndale's Friend

At dead of night standing at the quayside
Thomas Poyntz awaited the incoming tide
At last a small vessel slid in and docked
Its secret cargo in chests firmly locked.

Greeting the Captain, Poyntz then stepped back
As the contraband was loaded to a waiting trap.
Thomas pondered which was the safe route to take
To get his cargo to London before daybreak.

The Kings agents were looking everywhere
Bribing and plotting, the unwary to ensnare.
His friend William Tyndale had been betrayed
Now all reformers were very afraid.

Thomas Poyntz had risked all to save his friend
But in the end was forced to flee from Ostend.
He would honour his friend by spreading the word
In the new 'English' Bible wherever it could be heard.

Essex Man

Historical Note: *William Tyndale is credited with translating the bible from Hebrew into 'common' English and also the first to use the new medium of print. However his work brought him into conflict with the Anglican Church and Henry VIII. With his works banned Tyndale fled abroad. In 1536 whilst living in Antwerp he was captured by the King's agents and burned at the stake at Vilvoorde near Brussels. His last words were 'Lord, open the King of England's eyes'. Thomas Poyntz, Tyndale's friend was a North Ockendon merchant with business interests in Antwerp. He did his best to secure Tyndale's release but in the end had to flee to save his own life. However Poyntz arranged for some of the newly printed English bibles to be smuggled into England through Purfleet. The Poyntz family have a chapel in St. Mary Magdalene Church, North Ockendon.*

Dissolution

During vespers a messenger to Felsted came
With a letter addressed to the Abbot by name.
The King had proclaimed that Monasteries would be closed,
All their assets confiscated or otherwise disposed.

The Abbot called the Brothers to tell them the news
Grim faced he spoke slowly seeking their views.
One Monk enquired of the closure date.
The Abbot replied it won't be a long wait.

The monks dispersed to contemplate,
Pack possessions and await their fate.
Some remained in the chapel and prayed all night
For divine intervention to make things right.

All through the night there was an uneasy calm
Dawn came, nobody as yet had come to harm.
But just after noon four men beat on the door,
Then burst in with a taste of what was in store.

"I am Finch," swaggering in their leader said.
He slumped in the Abbots seat amid those he led.
"Leez Priory has a new owner by Royal Decree –
If you have any questions, then just ask me."

"In the name of Lord Rich," he said "I am proud,"
Finch's' cohorts looked at him and laughed out loud,
"With the blessing of the King to take ownership here
Together with farm, and all buildings near"

"You, you miserable man, get me some food
And wine, and women – I'm in the mood."
Finch's men rose and pushed the Abbot out
He understood then – the new authority was clout.

At sundown Lord Richard Rich arrived
Finch stood – "Good work I see you've survived."
Rich continued, "now then what have we got?"
"My Lord" said Finch, "you've got the lot!"

Andrew Summers

Historical Note: *The Augustinian Priory of Leez had originally been built in 1220 by Sir Ralph Gernon. Henry VIII ordered the dissolution of the Monasteries in England and Wales, citing lax morals and irregularities in them. However the main purpose was to boost Royal income. Between 1536 and 1540 nearly 800 were closed with many being sacked or sold at nominal prices to the Kings supporters. Waltham Abbey was the last Monastery to be dissolved. Lord Richard Rich was Chancellor of the Court of Augmentation, the body charged with diverting Monastic land for the crown. In the process Lord Rich acquired nearly 100 manors himself. Sir Richard later became Lord Rich of Leez and retired to the Priory where he built himself a grand new Tudor mansion. In his later years he tried to make up for earlier misdeeds by becoming a great benefactor to Felsted. Finch would have been one of Rich's 'enforcers' many of whom were used to save the Lord getting his hands dirty on such matters.*

PIE POWDER COURT SITTING

"Order Order. Is it the Mercer who is next?"
Richard Asser stood before the court looking vexed.
"The charge, false weights and measures my lord.
We have a witness here who will testify to the fraud?"

Looking up the Judge enquired, "Is this true?
Is this the first complaint or something new?"
"Sir, in Maldon Market it is the man's first offence
But *wherever* he goes he cheats by a few pence"

"Richard Asser, now do stand straight, how do you plead?
We take a dim view of those possessed by such greed" –
Guilty – "As I thought, bailiff seize the goods from his box
Then bring on the next case and send him to the stocks."

Andrew Summers

Historical Note: *This poem is based on records from a real case tried in 1566 in Maldon. Before the same court charges were brought against three shoemakers and two saddlers for displaying faulty goods. The term Pie Powder came from the Anglo-French pied-poudreux, meaning someone with dusty feet, such as itinerant merchants who toured the country to buy and sell at fairs. The courts died out in the nineteenth century but could be said to be the forerunner of present day trading standards.*

HARBINGERS AT HARLOW

The trumpeters sounded and pealing church bells
Announced the arrival of good Bess, their Queen.
Outriders in scarlet and gold spangled livery
Heralded such sights before never seen.

The crowds from Latton, Harlow and Netteswell
Awaited with joy this royal procession
With 500 courtiers expected to visit
And stay at Mark Hall for a wondrous progression.

After the heralds the Queen rode on horseback
Not for her the confines of a bumpy coach ride
With her fine gold hair glinting in sunlight
What a vision she looked with the Earl by her side.

The harbingers had left with their endless demands
Some walls to come down and others be painted
Swarming over the Hall giving measured commands
For perfection with which the Queen was acquainted.

James Altham and Dame Mary Judd were the hosts
But mingled with honour - the cost of it all!
Fish, game and fruit, brewed beer and wine
All were delivered and served at Mark Hall.

Payments to bakers, carpenters and labourers
The gift of a jewel or a sumptuous gown
This proud pair provided all fit for a Queen
Such was the sway and the power of the Crown.

Shirley Baker

Historical Note: *Every spring and summer Queen Elizabeth I went with her court on a 'Royal Progress' - to see and be seen by her people. Between 1571 and 1578 the Queen made three visits to Mark Hall in Harlow as the guest of James Altham and Mary Judd. The 'harbingers' were an advance party that inspected the accommodation, ensuring it was good enough for the Queen. Meeting their high standards could involve the host in considerable expense, in some cases spelling financial hardship. Hence a modern usage of the term in 'harbingers of doom.' Mark Hall has long since been demolished however there is a memorial to James Altham and Mary Judd in Saint Mary-at-Latton Church.*

A Weak and Feeble Woman

At the great military camp by Tilbury's Fort,
Long before the town became a major port,
Waited patiently more than twenty thousand troops
Guarding the small boats where the river loops.

The Queen rode up, a marshal's baton in her hand
Clad in armour on her charger, she came to a stand.
The Earls of Essex and Leicester held the bridle-rein
And Elizabeth, to her soldiers, spoke most plain.

"This day of the 9th of August 1588, let tyrants fear"
The Queen spoke loudly with a passion all could hear.
"I am come amongst you not for recreation or sport,"
The soldiers edged forward so every word was caught.

"I know I have the body of a weak and feeble woman,"
The nobles looked on as the Queen began
And all those kneeling rose as one to stand,
"But I have the heart and stomach of a king of England."

Angrily she poured scorn on those who would dare invade
Then dismounted after unleashing such a fearful tirade.
Filled with patriotic energy the Soldiers, a sight to be seen,
Stood with weapons raised heartily cheering their Queen.

Andrew Summers

Historical Note: *Queen Elizabeth addressed the troops at Tilbury shortly after the threat from the Spanish armada had been neutralised. The Armada with 130 ships and 30,000 men sailed from Lisbon on May 28, 1588. A combination of superior English tactics, ships, good intelligence, weather and luck had defeated the Armada by July 29th. As the prospect of invasion receded most of the troops at Tilbury were withdrawn in late August. The Armada finally limped home in the mid-September having lost half the fleet and most of its men.*

THE FATHER OF ENGLISH MUSIC?

William Byrd was a musical phenomenon
Throughout Europe acknowledged supreme.
Without him musicians, from Elgar to Elton,
Would not have known where to begin

In Queen Elizabeth's Royal Chapel he worked
For twenty-one years, enjoying royal favour.
Whatever the occasion he never shirked
Creating music both sacred and secular.

At fifty he retired from the chapel to dwell
Near his wealthiest patron Sir John Petrie,
Sheriff of Essex and first Lord of Writtle
He was Catholic, cultured, loved music as well.

Sir John's family seat was Ingatestone Hall.
Where Catholic services were secretly attested
Byrd played his settings of Latin mass for all
Behind closed doors to avoid being arrested.

'Stondon Place', became the Byrd family home,
Close to Ingatestone in Stondon Massey,
For thirty years till his life came to a close.
After, some say, his finest music was composed.

John Debenham

Historical note: *William Byrd (1539-1623) is considered by many as the greatest English composer of any age and with Palestrina and Orlando de Lassus, one of the great masters of the late renaissance. To be a Catholic in those times was dangerous but his talent and reputation earned him royal protection. Byrd bought Stondon Place, part of the manor of Stondon Massey, in 1593 and lived there until his death. The Stondon Place of today was rebuilt in 1878 after being destroyed by fire in 1877. Ingatestone Hall is a sixteenth century manor house built by Sir William Petrie Father of Sir John. Queen Elizabeth stayed there in 1561. Still owned and lived in by the Petrie family, the house, some half-mile from the village, is open to the public.*

Timeline

Essex Event commemorated	Year	National or International Event
	1603	*Queen Elizabeth I dies*
Harwich granted Royal Charter	1604	*William Shakespeare writes Othello*
Canvey Dutch Cottage Built	1618	*Sir Walter Raleigh is executed*
Ninth Family Group Join Mayflower	1620	*Pilgrim Fathers leave Plymouth*
Death of Billericay Pioneers	1621	*James I dies, Charles I is King*
Rev Dillingham completes 511 Wedding ceremonies in Sandon near Chelmsford	1635	*The speed of the Hackney carriage is set in London at 3mph*
Smuggling in Leigh on Sea continues	1642	*English Civil War starts*
Matthew Hopkins charges Elizabeth Clarke of Manningtree with Witchcraft	1644	*Abel Tasman maps north coast of Australia (New Holland)*
Roundheads lay siege to Colchester	1648	*Parliament tries Charles I for treason.*
	1649	*King Charles executed*
Samuel Pepys visits Audley End	1659	*Richard Cromwell resigns*
	1660	*Charles II returns from exile*
Richard Haddock commands 'Royal James'	1672	*Battle of Southwold Bay: 3rd Anglo-Dutch Naval War until 1674*
Samuel Pepys elected as MP for Harwich	1685	*Judge Jeffreys holds Bloody Assizes*
Daniel Defoe opens Brickworks	1694	*Bank of England is founded*
Daniel Defoe jailed for sedition	1703	*Death of Samuel Pepys*
Death of Sir Richard Haddock	1715	*Jaccobite revolt put down*
Birth of Dick Turpin	1705	*Construction of Blenheim Palace*
Walton Tower Built	1721	*Robert Walpole becomes the first prime minister of Britain*
Fairlop Fair begins in earnest	1725	*Black Watch founded in Scotland*
First recorded race at Galleywood	1770	*Birth of Poet William Wordsworth*
Tide Mill contructed at Battlesbridge	1775	*American Revolution begins*
Crown acquires Gunpowder Factory at Waltham Abbey	1775	*James Watt's builds prototype steam engine*
Essex & Kent 'Cricket' Match Tilbury	1776	*Declaration of Independence USA*
Richard Rigby investigated	1781	*First Building Society, in Birmingham.*
Lifeboat models first tested in Great Dunmow	1784	*Benjamin Franklin invents bifocals*
John Constable leaves Dedham school	1793	*Louis XVI of France executed*
Chelmer Navigation fully opened	1797	*Nore and Spithead Naval mutinies*
Sir Eliab Harvey takes command of the Essex Sea Fencibles	1798	*Irish Insurrection defeated*

Canvey Dutch Cottage

Wooden clogs wait on the fender
As though their owners still live here.

A clock ticks on the mantle piece
As if to take us back in time
To when canvas was at the window
And straw and seashells on the floor
Absorbed the encroaching water;
When fat-tailed sheep grazed
The low-lying lands
And were milked to make
A bitter cheese.

Much of Canvey's history
Unfolded before this sturdy cott
Some brides caught malaria and died
Within months of coming here;
Bare-knuckled fighters planned their fights
When the only policeman went once a year
To the mainland
His lamp stands on the cottage shelf
A reminder of those illicit times.

The flood of 1953 came to its door
But still the octagonal walls stood firm
A tribute to Vermuyden's skilful past
Designed by this Dutchman - built to last.

Shirley Baker

Historical Note: *The cottage, built in 1618, is a legacy from the Dutch occupation of Canvey in the 17th century. Cornelius Vermuyden, who was commissioned to drain the Fens in East Anglia, also worked on flood barriers at Dagenham. However he left a lasting legacy on Canvey Island. Three hundred Dutchmen worked on the Canvey Sea defences and land reclamation work. They were in part paid by land grants from the area reclaimed. More recently, before becoming a museum the cottage housed a family of eight and also served as a tea shop prior to the 1960s.*

Billericay Pioneers

Christopher Martin and wife Marie headed the ninth family group
With Solomon Prower and John Langmore,
The Billericay Pioneers in their little troop.

They abandoned their roots for a New World life,
Fleeing persecution and intolerance which under
King James rule was rife.

Christopher Martin organised victuals and supplies
In the knowledge that once they were gone
He would sever all his Essex ties.

At the start of the voyage the Pilgrims numbered 102,
Together on the Mayflower with common beliefs
And a shared point of view.

Andrew Summers

***Historical Note:** On September 6th 1620, the Mayflower, with the Pilgrim Fathers, left Plymouth after much delay. The ship's captain was Christopher Jones from Harwich. Landfall was made on November 11th 1620. Sixty six days had been spent at sea and 2750 nautical miles had been travelled. One new 'Pilgrim' was born on the voyage and one died. Sadly though, of the original 102 Pilgrims, half had died within three months of arrival in America, including all the pioneers from Billericay.*

Say 'I do,' Pay the Fee, Sign the Book

Rector Gilbert Dillingham, in King James' reign,
Thought of a scheme for financial gain.
Promoting weddings; 'no questions asked,'
He had customers heading his way fast.

Lovesick grooms and would be brides
Headed to Sandon from far and wide.
Not wanting to travel to Gretna Green
Their nuptials there to rapidly convene.

He married the daughter of a neighbouring vicar
To get the ceremony over that much quicker.
The false name she gave was the one he took;
'Just pay the fee, say I do and sign the book.'

The Reverend conducted weddings this way
Sending many happy couples on their way.
For twenty years behind St Andrews church door,
Twenty-five times a year; up from merely four.

The Reverend retiring brought an end to this scam
Brian Walton, the new Rector, was an honest man.
He took a very dim view of what had gone before
And Sandon's 'Quickie' weddings would be no more.

Andrew Summers

Historical Note: *It is not known what happened to The Reverend Dillingham in his retirement. Brian Walton became rector of Sandon in 1636 when Charles I was on the throne and was caught up in the political turmoil of the time. He lost the rectorship of Sandon and then was imprisoned in 1641. Undeterred on release, and a committed Royalist, he survived the English Civil War and Cromwell. At the Restoration he was made chaplain to King Charles II and in 1660 enthroned as Bishop of Chester.*

Leigh Fishy Tales.

With its history as steep as its Church Hill Lane,
Leigh-on-Sea guards its heroes and ghosts just the same.
The pressgang, that old eighteenth century scourge,
Would wait by the church for the men to emerge
From prayer on the Sabbath and bar their way home
Having sharpened their swords on the 'Cutlass stone'.
A family of Haddocks all served the Crown.
The 'Crooked Billet' was their house of renown.
Old Captain Haddock, while fighting Dutch wars,
Stopped their fifty gun galleons from rounding the Nore.
Such maritime heritage is Leigh's warp and weft.
Secret 'Peter Boat' passages are all that is left
Of the smuggling trade that brought 'baccy' and rum,
Flemish lace for the ladies and tea by the drum,
To be taken by cart across Dawes Heath at dawn,
Bound for London, avoiding the Excise, guns drawn.
From captains to cockles, these tales still amaze.
If you listen, they're still being whispered today.

Karen Bowman

Historical Note: *The table gravestone in Leigh Churchyard is worn down and carries strange cut marks and is thought to have been where the pressgang waited for the men of Leigh to leave church so as to press them into service. Members of the Salmon, Haddock and Goodlad families were among those who served from Leigh in the Dutch wars of the Seventeenth and Eighteenth centuries. Captain William Haddock lived from 1607 – 1667. His son Admiral William Haddock became comptroller of the navy, while Robert Salmon and William Goodlad both became Masters of Trinity House. Smugglers used secret passages, some supposedly under The 'Peter Boat' public house, to bring contraband ashore and then it was taken over nearby Dawes Heath to London in shrimp carts.*

Witnesses in White

With elegant long necks and stately progress
The swans in numbers glide,
From Manningtree to Mistley
Along the river Stour both clear and wide.

How many generations have there been
To forage and feed upon the brewery out-fall
Were they there when Mathew first was seen?
Did they act as witnesses silent and aloof?

Mathew Hopkins the Witch Finder General in 1644
With his assistant Stearne persecuted more
Than two hundred through several counties.

An oak tree stands still, where the last witch was hung
In sight of that river running free
Was a swan song for her then sung?
Or were the witnesses white and mute?

There were seven or eight in a windy March
Accused by him – especially four –
Who made "Solemn sacrifices offered to the Devil"
And were he said "with hatred filled for him"

Elizabeth Clarke was hung after the Assizes of 1644
Three others there were and then there were more.
Nineteen all told had been pricked and swum
In the cold, cold waters with the shining bird.

Margaret Rice 1934 - June 2006

Historical Note: *Mathew Hopkins perhaps the most famous Witch Finder General appointed himself to the post. Over 200 executions for witchcraft were carried out during his tenure. Many of the victims were taken to Colchester Castle and tortured in the dungeons. It was a time when the English Civil War was raging and Hopkins took advantage of the climate of religious intolerance and chaos that existed to pursue his grisly task.*

UNDER SIEGE

On the ninth of June they invaded the town
Things in their way just got knocked down.
Lucas and Lisle had the Royalist command,
We waited in fear of the invaders demands.

They took our homes, set up defensive positions,
Whatever they needed was simply requisitioned.
They broke into our stores and stole our food,
Those offering resistance were roughly subdued.

Imprisoned in our own town with no way out
We spent days, lying low in a filthy dugout
The constant bombardment never slows
And the pace of the battle daily grows.

Roundhead cannon destroy the town bit by bit
Its citizens trapped since the Royalists seized it.
People not killed by the attacking fire
Starve to death, there's no food to acquire.

The Roundhead noose tightens, the Royalists despair
Hunger and death stalk everywhere
They scavenge: We scavenge; all cupboards are bare,
There is no salvation except in prayer.

John Debenham

Historical Note: *Towards the end of the English Civil War, the Earl of Norwich one of the King's supporters crossed into Essex with a force of about 3000 men, following defeat at Maidstone. He headed for Colchester and occupied the town. Most of the citizens of Colchester were trapped inside. Lord General Fairfax commanding the parliamentary forces encircled the town after a few brief skirmishes. For eleven weeks in the summer of 1648 Colchester was under siege. With starvation at hand and no prospect of relief the Royalists surrendered. Two Royalist commanders Sir Charles Lucas and Sir George Lisle were summarily executed. During the siege extensive damage was inflicted upon Colchester with nearly a quarter of its housing destroyed.*

DEAR DIARY

Up at four o'clock and after I got ready
With Mr Blayton, took horse and rode steady
To Saffron Walden where at The White Hart
The landlord took us on foot through the park

To view Audley End House in its beautiful grounds
The whole of the place could not be better found.
The stately interior, so exceeding worth seeing,
The layout and style, the chimney-pieces and ceilings.

Down in the cellar, there being excellent sound
I played my flageolette which echoed all round,
Then, a most admirable drink being served
A health to the king, we thought was deserved.

Being shewn two pictures that should not be missed,
'Henry the Eighth', and one of 'The Four Evangelists'.
Our tour was nearly over; our guide had served us well
So with two shillings for his trouble, we bad him farewell.

Andrew Summers

Historical Note: *Samuel Pepys (1633 - 1703) recorded his visit to Audley End in his diary in 1659. Two abridged volumes of his original diaries are kept in the Library. The estate was given to Lord Audley by Henry VIII after he dissolved the abbey which stood on the site. Thomas Howard, Ist Earl of Suffolk a descendant of Lord Audley, commissioned the house which when built in 1614 was the largest house in England. During World War II the house was used by the Special Operations Executive (SOE) for training Polish Agents. A flageolette (flageolet) is a wind instrument somewhat similar to the flute, and closely related to the recorder.*

Elected by 32

In 1604 King James granted as never before
A Charter for Harwich as the basis of local law.
It made the town, with a wealth of new power,
A borough where local government would flower.

Honest, good and wholesome rules were needed
As the will of the council was not to be impeded.
Aldermen and Councillors were expected to be discreet
And removed only if guilty of misdemeanour and deceit.

This body approved by the King, held office for life
Although changes could be made in times of civil strife.
Elections were not considered suitable at that stage
And as for public opinion, that was impossible to gauge.

A Mayor was picked from within the ruling group
And any new councillors had to be in a privileged loop.
With responsibility for police, courts, a jail and fines to collect
The council had also two Members of Parliament to elect!

Andrew Summers

Historical Note: *Harwich celebrated the 400th anniversary of its Royal Charter in 2004. Two of its most famous Members of Parliament were Samuel Pepys and Sir Anthony Deane, who were elected in 1685 by the town council (total votes 32). Harwich was truly a 'Rotten' borough.*
A series of reform acts in 1832, 1835 and 1868 abolished the 'Rotten' boroughs and reduced Harwich's representation to 1 MP. In 1859, 317 names were listed on the electoral register for Harwich and Dovercourt, although this had risen to nearly 10,000 by 1910.

The Brick Maker of Chadwell St Mary

In 1694 Daniel Defoe was doing well.
His factory made tiles and bricks to sell.
Living in Chadwell in a big house of note
With his own coach, footman and pleasure boat.

At times more than 100 men worked on site,
But their pay was low as Defoe was quite tight.
What was worse any ruffian who came passing by
Was taken on without reference and given a try.

Defoe didn't pay proper attention to his charge
Resulting in complaints from customers at large.
The tiles were alleged to be quite porous
Not weatherproof - was the resounding chorus.

Then came a lawsuit over the supply of beer,
Which rocked the course he was trying to steer.
In reality Defoe's attention to detail had strayed
He was preoccupied, and for this he dearly paid.

Defoe's writings were attacking establishment views
Accused of sedition, brought to court he made news.
Though enjoying some support, still he was jailed.
Worse was to come, then his brick factory failed

Essex Man

Historical Note: *Daniel Defoe was brick maker, novelist, journalist and pamphleteer. He spent nine years in Tilbury. Born in 1660 in Cripplegate, London, he was the son of a butcher, James Foe. Daniel Defoe's most famous novel 'Robinson Crusoe' was published in 1719. He also wrote 'Moll Flanders' in 1722 which was partly set in Colchester. Defoe was credited with publishing over 560 books and pamphlets and considered by some to be the founder of British journalism. He died in 1731.*

Stand and Deliver

"Stand and Deliver," these words of dread
Dick Turpin is reputed once to have said.
An ex-apprentice who cheated and lied,
A killer and thief whose threats terrified.

He began his career with local petty crime
Graduating to rustling and smuggling in time,
Hiding in Epping he often laid low
Plotting with his gang where to strike the next blow.

One Saturday night the gang came with stealth
To Widow Shelley's house to steal her wealth.
They threatened murder saying, "where's your gold?"
Then they held her over a fire till she told.

A reward by the London Evening Post
Was publicised widely from city to coast
The hunt intensified throughout the county
To catch the villains and claim the bounty.

With the net closing in, the gang knew no rest
And with nowhere to hide fled to the forest.
There they fell out, as thieves do quite unplanned,
Signalling the end of their unsavoury band.

To York Turpin fled where his first crime did fail,
Caught in the act he was sent straight to jail.
Traced by a letter to his brother he'd penned,
At Knavesmire gallows Dick Turpin met his end.

Andrew Summers

***Historical Note:** Dick Turpin was born in Hempstead in 1705. In real life he was totally devoid of glamour and was hanged as a common criminal at Knavesmire, York in 1739. The legend was created through the popular 1834 novel 'Rookwood.' written by Harrison Ainsworth. Turpin's fictitious great ride north was based on a real life 17th-century highwayman John 'Swift Nick' Nevison who covered more than 190 miles on horseback in just 15 hours.*

Dick Turpin

Walton Tower

Through the mist we see you now
A column of unchanging certainty
WaltonTower blesses us in our sights
As we sail hard across the sea.

Over 'Prebenda Consumpta' we come
Oh can we hear those sunken bells?
Well hidden now beneath the sea
And only in tales that history tells.

The coffins floated back to land
To be caught by villagers waiting there
And many a table, many a chair
Were fashioned on shore by eager hands.

We may not hear the bells that tolled
Nor see the smugglers secret works
But know full well the waves that rolled
Helped them in their shameful perks.

So now we've sailed the Northern Sea
And safely we've come home
Guided by that Walton Tower
We'll rest before we roam.

But after, we will cast off again
Through Backwaters find our way
The battle calls us and we'll fight
Through many another day.

Shirley Baker

Historical Note: *Once known as Eadolfenaesse and also Waltonia, the town of Walton now takes its name from the Naze, the area of headland known for its ancient fossils, unique wildlife and its ongoing battle against the sea. For the last 250 years the headland has been dominated by the Naze Tower, built in 1721 by Trinity House. Its original purpose was to act as a marker for ships approaching the Harwich harbour, a duty it still performs today. The tower has also played a part in the many wars since the 18th century. Believed to be the only Tower of its kind in the world, it has recently been refurbished and opened as a visitor attraction.*

The old Parish Church of All Saints belonging to the Diocesan estate of St Paul's Cathedral, now called 'Prebenda Consumpta per Mare' was washed away completely in 1796 a victim of coastal erosion. The sea has advanced several hundred feet from where it once stood.

The Walton Backwaters provided the inspiration for Arthur Ransom's famous children's adventure story 'Swallow and Amazons'.

THE FAIRLOP FRIGATE

Daniel Day was accident prone, road travel made him quiver
A keen sailor he was much more at home floating on the river.
Needing to cross East London to get to Fairlop Fair
He came up with a solution that would get him there.

The Fairlop Frigate came from Wapping by road
Leading up front a full marching band strode
Through Bow, then Stratford and Ilford it passed
With crowds lining the route and staring aghast.

The Frigate was a six-horse-drawn vessel on wheels
A real fully rigged warship from crow's-nest to keels
With its flags and banners, this odd thing marine
Trundling through East London a sight to be seen.

Daniel Day sat proudly amongst his guests.
Maybe forty accompanying him, all well dressed.
Sitting under the great oak at Fairlop Fair
Eating bacon and beans and other fine fare.

Andrew Summers

Historical Note: *In the 1720 Daniel Day founder of the Fair inherited some property near Fairlop and collected the rents annually on the first Friday in July. After the collection he enjoyed a beanfeast with friends under the ancient Fairlop Oak. By 1725 others joined in and the gathering took on the appearance of a Fair, with sales of trinkets, toys, ribbons and entertainments such as puppets, circus acrobats and wild beasts. Ten years later there were several prosecutions of stallholders for gaming and illegal sales of liquor. In the 1750's over 100,000 people attended the Fair from all over London. At times the fair became so rowdy it had to be closed. In 1793 the Fair was banned after a riot and what was described as great encouragement of vice and immorality. The Fair continued for another 100 years or more, despite the loss of The Oak in a gale in 1820 and deforestation in 1851 when most of the area was converted into farmland.*
Daniel Day died in 1767, aged 84 buried in a coffin fashioned from a huge branch from the Fairlop Oak.

THE QUEEN'S PLATE

Stock Road was shut, hotels and inns were full.
School closed as race day exerted its pull.
Feverish, excited crowds eagerly waited
To glimpse the jockeys and guess how they rated.

Thousands descended upon the course,
To place a bet on their favourite horse.
Men beavered away to get the track ready,
The ground prepared and hurdles made steady.

Inn keepers tried to satisfy unquenchable thirst,
Bookmakers challenged punters to do their worst.
One or two local farmers looked somewhat peeved,
Seeing their workers there - absent without leave.

Prizefighters squared up, without their coats.
Fighting cocks clawed at each other's throats.
In contrast gentlemen paraded in their best
Escorting their ladies so elegantly dressed.

The Queen Charlotte Plate, so much at stake,
A hundred guinea purse for the winner to take.
Horses and riders, each eyeing the opposition
Eager for the start, they jostle for position.

THEY'RE OFF, past the Eagle, the course three miles long
Goes over the road then turns south, so far nothing wrong.
Then thundering back at a pace that could kill
Past the Admiral Rous, round the church, up the hill

To the grandstand by Watchhouse Road they come,
Four-year-old mares, hearts straining for home.
The first past the post receives a great cheer;
Winning punters collect, losers cry in their beer.

Art Szmauz

Historical Note: *The earliest recorded racing event in Galleywood was in 1770. King George III gave permission for the year's main event to be called the Queen's Plate, in honour of his wife, Queen Charlotte, who first set foot on English soil in Essex. The Galleywood course was the longest race course in Britain and the only one to circle a church. After many ups and downs racing ended in 1935. Chelmsford Borough Council bought much of the land around the Grandstand for housing after World War II. White fencing still marks some of the course along Stock Road.*

Three Mills at Battlesbridge

Here, the confluence of centuries –
Three mills –
Three histories of quern and staple –
Ground from their meaning by the tides of traffic.

One whose wheels were overshot by time –
Now but the grist for powder-paint and palette.

Three mills –
Three moments in the mystery of grain –
Steeped in the engine of revolving light.

One who knew of vacuum and steam-
Of spritsails that are ghosted by the quay.

Here, the confluence of centuries –
Three Mills –
Three entries in the register of man –
Bound to the landscape by the chaff of seasons.

The last a husk of broken steel and weeds –
Now obsolete in dust and dereliction.

Mervyn Linford

Historical Note: *In 1775 a tide mill was constructed on the south bank of the River Crouch at Battlesbridge. It was not a successful venture and the mill burnt down in 1815. In 1896 William Meeson from Grays built a steam powered mill on the north bank which was also damaged by fire in 1926. Lastly in 1933 a feed mill was constructed on the south bank. This mill was originally gas fired. Battlesbridge is now home to the largest antique centre in Essex.*

It's Not Cricket!

It should have been a real fine game
When Kent and Essex county teams came
To play a one day match at Tilbury Fort
But that day shame to cricket was brought.

The teams took to the field to begin the contest
When objections to a Kentish man lead to unrest.
His team became angry tempers began to fray,
Essex withdrew from the field and refused to play.

A Kent player took exception to this silly attitude
Seized a gun from the guardhouse and started a feud.
Onlookers were shocked when an Essex man was shot
Then mayhem ensued with all cricketing rules forgot.

Both teams ran to the armoury attacking the guard
Grabbing all sorts of weapons they fought in the yard.
One guard was bayoneted and the sergeant shot dead
Before Kent took to their boats and the Essex men fled.

Andrew Summers

Historical Note: *The substance of this story was in a letter from Gravesend published in the London Chronicle on 31st October 1776. The account remained unchallenged for 200 years when its authenticity was questioned especially as the match was supposed to have taken place at the end of October. Essex County cricket Club was formed in 1876 at Brentwood moving to Chelmsford in 1966. One hundred and three years later, in 1979, Essex won their first major trophies - the County Championship and the Benson & Hedges Cup. Happily there have been no repeats of the match of 1776.*

Rigbys' Follies

Beside the Stour two towers stand,
Relics of a scheme to make Mistley grand,
The Swan Fountain a little further to the east
Is all that's left since planned work ceased.

Richard Rigby saw his reinvented family seat
As a spa town on the river to attract the elite.
Architect Robert Adams received the commission
To bring this project to its full fruition.

Building on this scale required major investment
Lots of Rigby's money and long term commitment.
But the source of his fortune, to some, was suspect
So where it came from was rigorously checked.

Caught up in the scandal of 'The Naze Tea Room'
Now shady accounting was to seal Rigby's doom.
Paymaster in the American Revolutionary War
With access to vast funds which he oversaw.

It was only a matter of time until he went
With differences in income and what he spent.
Disgraced, out of office, lucky not be jailed
His funds all gone, his great dream failed.

Andrew Summers

Historical note: *Richard Rigby was Paymaster of the Forces between 1768 and 1782. A report by the House of Commons, Commissioners of Public Accounts in 1781 "Urged immediate action to impose checks on the money held at any one time by the Paymaster whilst in office, and to prevent those leaving office from taking large sums of public money with them".*
Part of Richard Adam's church at Mistley was demolished in 1870, when the new parish church in New Road was built. The Architects best surviving works can be seen at Syon House, Osterly and Admiralty Arch. The Naze Tower Scandal involved clandestine rendezvous, between actresses and gentlemen in high government places, at the then tearoom.

At The Doctor's Pond

Lionel Lukin from Dunmow, had scientific taste,
He was forever inventing, often in great haste.
Favoured by Royalty, with friends in high places,
His creations always impressed the right faces.

Lukin began as a fashionable coach maker;
But he liked the challenge of being a risk taker.
One day the War Office issued a new request
Which inspired Lukin to work without rest.

In a long detailed paper the following was asked,
And a very tight timetable with penalties tasked.
'We want an improved method of construction of a boat
That if filled with water will still stay afloat.'

Lukin set to work with an unrelenting zeal.
He built two models with amazing appeal.
Each made of wood with strong glue to bond,
To test them, off he went to the Doctor's Pond

Under weeping willows, the models were tested
With the ducks, escorting them quite interested.
All Saturday he spent playing with his toys
To the great delight of little girls and boys.

"Hello, hello, what's going on?" from a constable passing by-
"Shoosh National Security" said Lukin splashing "I cannot lie".
Mad, but harmless thought the officer who took no action -
The models didn't sink - ducks flying away the only reaction.

Art Szmauz

Historical Note: *The Doctor's Pond in Great Dunmow was the scene of the first 'unsinkable' lifeboat experiments in 1784. Lionel Lukin worked till the age of 82. Further tests of full size vessels were carried out on the Thames and off Ramsgate. Lukin spent his whole life resisting claims from others that it was their invention. However Lukin rests with words 'Inventor of the lifeboat principle' inscribed on his gravestone. It is said the Doctor's Pond gets its name from a Doctor who bred and kept leeches there for medical purposes.*

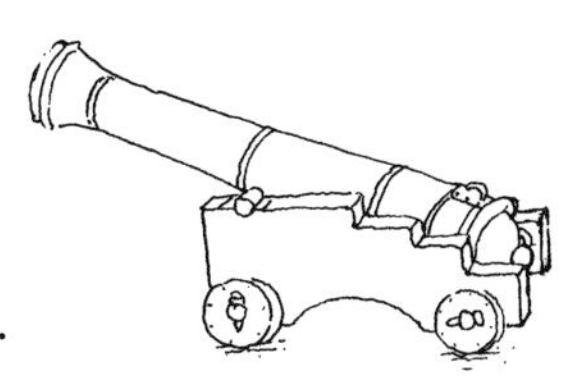

GUNPOWDER'S LOT

In old naval days many phrases came to be
Such as some of the following as we shall see.

A LOOSE CANNON is perhaps someone out of control
or when the pitch of the sea could cause a gun to roll.
An unfair term maybe, but a bit of a rogue was the SON OF A GUN
The result of the parents on deck having their illicit fun.

Stuff the barrel was the master gunner's wish
using old rope - unwanted items or rubbish.
It was needed to stop a cannon ball falling into the sea,
So A LOAD OF JUNK found, was the key.

FLASH IN THE PAN was failure after a showy start.
It could be fatal in battle on the crew's part.
In which case OVER A BARREL was a situation helpless,
Or a crewman flogged for creating such a mess.

HANG FIRE – delayed an action.
Not always recommended as danger results from inaction.
Thus STICK TO YOUR GUNS and maintain your position
Don't change your mind, it's time to make a decision.

BRASS MONKEYS is a term for the extreme cold.
The brass racks would contract, the cannon balls no longer hold.
And HOISTED BY ONE'S OWN PETARD was the end
Blown sky high by the device made ready to defend.

Andrew Summers

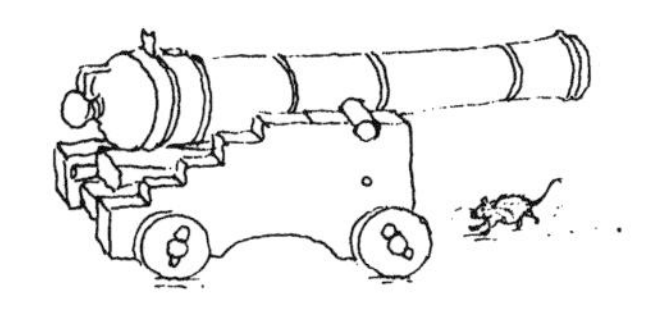

Historical Note: *Most of the above sayings originate from the navy and its use of gunpowder and cannon in warfare. The Gunpowder Mills at Waltham Abbey were originally a private company, but acquired by the Crown in 1787. For 200 years the Mills worked on the development and manufacture of gunpowder and explosives. At its apogee during the first world war 5000 people worked in the factory.*

John Constable's School Days

Every day young John would walk to school,
Observing the countryside as an absolute jewel.
Along the banks, across the fields or leafy lanes,
In snow or Summer's heat or the wet from the rains.

Every trip brought something new
A cloud, an insect, a wild bird or simply the morning dew.
The seasons passed and colours changed,
The land was golden when harvest was arranged.

To arrive at Dedham School he crossed the county line.
Supervised strictly by Dr Grimwood, the student would be fine.
John Constable met many new people and developed his skill
In later life he would produce his masterpieces on Flatford Mill.

Andrew Summers

Historical note: *John Constable (1776 -1837), England's greatest landscape painter would have walked to school each day from East Bergholt in Suffolk, where he lived, to the Old Grammar School in Dedham. Constable attended school there until the age of 17. Dedham School is now a private house. John Constable also painted a number of views of Hadleigh Castle. One painted in 1829 can be seen in Tate Britain.*

Waterway to Chelmsford

Maldon was a big port, Chelmsford a small town.
Maldon didn't want a canal; afraid of trade going down.
But men of vision financed it, they took the long view
Richard Coats and his navvies drove the canal through.

Coal, iron and lime, stone, grain and sugar,
Were some of the cargoes the barges delivered
To Chelmsford direct from Heybridge basin,
And the town grew fast with this waterborne invasion.

Gasworks, sugar factory, water driven mills,
Iron founders, stone masons, potters with their kilns.
Horse drawn barges kept them all supplied.
Creating opportunities, the whole area thrived.

Sixty thousand tons were carried in its busiest year
But in 1843 the bargees had much to fear.
The railway came and trade began to diminish.
In 1960 the horses went, by '72 trade was finished.

No longer featuring in Chelmsford's news
No cargoes to Heybridge, dodging Maldon port dues.
The canal now only plays host to the pleasure
That waterway enthusiasts of all tastes treasure.

John Debenham

Historical note: *The Canal was built, and is still owned and operated by, 'The Company of The Proprietors of the Chelmer and Blackwater Navigation Limited'. Fully opened in 1797, its last commercial cargo was in 1972, with horse-drawn traffic until 1960. After playing a major role in Chelmsford's growth, the canal is still in use for pleasure-craft.*

HARVEY'S ESSEX SEA FENCIBLES

An icy wind sliced through the bleak quay,
Storm clouds gathered over an angry sea.
On the jetty 20 men shivered in the cold
Waiting patiently to do as they were told.

"Fall in you miserable lot –
Let's show the commander what we've got.
LOOK SHARP! – OFFICER ON DECK – TEN SHUN!
Chin up, watch me, this is the ways it's done."

Sir Eliab Harvey arrived in his naval barge,
On tour to inspect the men in his charge.
He looked splendid in his pressed uniform,
His buttons glistening in the gathering storm.

The motley group looked a pathetic sight,
Shuffling, trying their best to stand upright.
The commander stepped ashore
Quickly absorbing what he saw.

Raising his voice "You there, who are you?"
"Harris; Thomas Sir, Essex Sea Fencibles, I'm new."
"Well Thomas Harris what do you do, pray tell?"
"Bait digging, Sir," Harris beamed, "which I do very well."

Eliab Harvey looked them in the eye and began
"You are the First Sea Fencibles of Essex, every man.
Each and every one of you," he continued most intense.
"Are our eyes and ears, essential for our coastal defence."

Essex Man

Historical Note: *The Sea Fencibles were a nautical Home Guard. Each man was a part time volunteer paid one shilling a day. Sir Eliab Harvey from Chigwell commanded the Essex Sea Fencibles from 1798 to 1799 at a time when invasion by Napoleon was most feared. Harvey was also an Essex MP. However his main claim to fame was as Captain of the 'Temeraire' at the Battle of Trafalgar. Eliab Harvey was one of the pall bearers at Lord Nelson's funeral.*

HARVEY'S SEA FENCIBLES REPORTING FOR DUTY

Timeline

Essex Event commemorated	Year	National or International Event
Nave of Chelmsford Church Collapses	1800	*Britain occupies Malta.*
Eliab Harvey becomes Captain of The Temeraire	1803	*Henry Shrapnel invents the Shell*
Temeraire and Harvey at Trafalgar	1805	*Battle of Trafalgar*
Elizabeth Fry visits Newgate Prison	1810	*First public Billiard room opens in Covent Garden*
Arrival of James Murrel in Hadleigh	1812	*British PM Spencer Percival is assassinated in Parliament*
Excavation of Bartlow Hills	1815	*Battle of Waterloo*
Hard Apple arrested on Godwin Sands	1820	*Birth of Florence Nightingale*
John Constable paints Hadleigh Castle	1829	*Birth of Geronimo, Apache leader*
First Southend Wooden Pier opened	1830	*Last person put in pillory in England*
Machine Breakers Riot in Lt. Clacton	1831	*Belgium becomes independent*
Rotten Boroughs abolished	1832	*First Great Reform Act*
Alfred Lord Tennyson arrives in Epping	1837	*William IV dies, Victoria reigns.*
David Livingstone gets lost in Ongar	1838	*Public Record Office is established*
David Livingstone leaves for Africa	1840	*Queen Victoria marries Prince Albert*
Plum Puddings eaten at Romford Workhouse on Christmas Day	1841	*Britain claims sovereignty in Hong Kong*
Hockley Spa Pump Room Built	1843	*Dickens 'A Christmas Carol' published.*
Coggeshall Gang Strikes	1844	*YMCA founded in London*
Danbury Palace name adopted	1845	*Potato crop fails in Ireland*
HMS Warrior launched at Bow Golden age of the Thames Barge	1860	*Abraham Lincoln elected 16th US President*
Death of Sarah Moore Leigh Sea Witch	1867	*Dominion of Canada created*
Southend Watch Vessel No 7 scrapped	1870	*Death of Charles Dickens*
Coalhouse Fort East Tilbury completed	1874	*Disraeli becomes Prime Minister*
Essex County Cricket Club formed	1876	*Wyatt Earp arrives in Dodge City*
Epping Forest Act Passed	1878	*First electric street lights in London*
William Morris writes on Walthamstow	1883	*Buffalo Bill creates 'Wild West Show'*
Essex Earthquake	1884	*General Gordon besieged at Khartoum*
A.C. Wilkin, founds Tiptree Jam	1885	*The Statue of Liberty arrives in USA.*
Rev. Baring-Gould writes Onward, CS	1865	*Abraham Lincoln is assassinated*
Transfer of Essex villages of Ugley, Farnham and others to Herts resisted.	1888	*Jack the Ripper murders six women in London*
Southend Iron Pier opened	1889	*Cecil Rhodes obtains royal charter for British South Africa Company*
Creation of Kynocktown	1890	*Death of Vincent van Gogh*
Salvation Army Colony opened in Hadleigh	1891	*Edison patents movie camera*
Marconi sets up in Chelmsford	1895	*Birth of Buster Keaton*
Gilbey Accolade for Finchingfield	1898	*Paris Metro opened*

Grave Diggers

It was heavy dirty work to pull up the floor
But we were six strong men fit for the chore.
We were opening a vault as the last resting place
Of a man of means - Chelmsford his birthplace.

With great effort we lifted the flagstone
Then burrowed down into the unknown
We toiled away at the soil without a break
Our bodies heaving and starting to ache.

We took out the spoil removing loose bricks
Chipping round the column with our picks.
From first light we worked without pause all day
Deserving a break we had earned our pay.

To the Saracen's Head we went for refreshment
And after a jar or two of ale felt quite content.
Having just sat back we suddenly heard a great din
And somebody shouting "The roof's fallen in!"

We rushed out to see what was going on,
And saw that the whole church roof had gone.
The columns of the south arcade had collapsed
All the length of the nave right up to the apse!

Art Szmauz

Historical Note: *Church building began in Chelmsford in 1200 at the same time as the town itself was founded. The First Rector, was Roger de Gorges in 1242. The 'Parish Church' became a Cathedral in 1914 when the Diocese of Chelmsford was created. Later in 1954 its dedication was extended to include St Peter and St Cedd. The collapse of the church occurred on 17th January 1800 and careless digging was suspected. The South Isle, part of the North Isle, the pews and the west gallery were completely destroyed. Rebuilding took place almost immediately. Chelmsford Cathedral still hold the original 1801 bill for decoration of the replacement Georgian gothic ceiling in Naples yellow - some 13 guineas.*

THE LADY ON THE FIVE POUND NOTE

Told of the horrors facing women in prison life,
A mother of eight children and a good Quaker wife,
Elizabeth Fry went to see for herself in Newgate jail
Women crammed thirty to a cell, with no hope of bail.

Offenders of both serious and minor crime
Locked up together in squalor and grime.
Old, young, even babies, all in the same state,
In an unhygienic stench awaiting their fate.

Shocked and dismayed by the conditions she saw
She called for prison reform and change to the law.
Of the prison conditions there was official disregard
So Mrs Fry campaigned on, lobbying parliament hard.

She spoke to politicians, she spoke with the Queen.
To Prime ministers also she told what she had seen.
Newgate's school and chapel were small battles won,
In the rest of the country there was much to be done.

Travelling the country gathering evidence needed
Her pleas for reform were eventually heeded
And parliament came to see the need for revision
Of laws and rules governing conditions in prison.

John Debenham

Historical Note: *Elizabeth Fry worked tirelessly to improve prison and social conditions. In 1810 one hundred thousand people were in prison. (One third more than today) Over 200 crimes attracted the death penalty including shop lifting and forgery. As a result of Fry's campaigning prison conditions for women were improved and the number of capital offences gradually reduced. By 1861, only 4 capital crimes remained after the passing of the Criminal Law Consolidation Act of that year. Elizabeth Fry's work has been honoured by her depiction on the Bank of England £5.00 note since 1992. Living in Plashet (now East Ham) since her marriage in 1800, their original house stood in Plashet Park. A lifelong Quaker, Elizabeth Fry died on 12 October 1845. Although Quakers do not have funeral services over 1,000 people stood in silence as she was buried at 'The Society of Friends' graveyard in Barking.*

ONCE THERE WERE SEVEN

Near Ashdon, just three Bartlow Hills now stand
Hidden from view by trees on farmland.
A tall fence encloses the site, front to back,
With access on foot by a narrow muddy track.

Their Roman age secrets remained unseen
Until excavated in eighteen fifteen
Many relics were removed for short-term gain
To be sold for quick profit and not seen again.

Some items were saved and put into safe store
Until a disastrous fire burnt the place to its core.
Then Victorian railway builders arrived;
They flattened four Hills, but three have survived.

For a century these three lay forgotten and neglected
Before Essex County Council made the site protected.
The Railway long closed, county boundaries adjusted,
Now to Cambridgeshire, Bartlow Hills are entrusted.

Andrew Summers

Historical Note: *Bartlow Hills was originally the largest group of Roman barrows (artificial hills) in Northern Europe. The seven burial mounds contained a wealth of period materials and objects. Their steep conical shape is typical of the Roman era. The Bartlow Hills had become overgrown and in 1978 they were taken into care by Essex County Council. The site was cleared and fences built for protection. Twelve years later the Hills passed to Cambridgeshire County Council after a change in the County boundary. A number of the remaining artefacts and papers relating to site excavation can be found in Safron Waldon and Colchester Museums.*

Hard Apple.

William Blyth was a smuggler nicknamed 'Hard Apple'
With whom the Revenue for years tried to grapple.
A shopkeeper and Parish Councillor first rate,
He was also oysterman, constable and magistrate.

Being a prominent member of the community
Gave him a certain amount of immunity.
He enjoyed the double life of shifting contraband
Whilst administering 'justice' on the other hand.

Blyth came from a colourful family of yore
Whose cupboards might yield up skeletons galore.
He'd bring back from Dunkirk on his boat 'Big Jane',
Illicit gin and tobacco to be sold for gain.

A revenue cutter one-day drew along side
Customs men boarded in a routine well tried.
The smugglers plied their pursuers with drink
Leaving them befuddled and unable to think.

'Hard Apple' was once arrested on the high sea
By John Loten a customs official from Leigh,
The boat ran aground, Loten and prisoner were stuck
Till a storm blew up bringing the smuggler luck.

Trapped on Goodwin Sands; the boat could be lost,
Loten had no choice, which would be to his cost.
He unchained his prisoner, to be free from captivity
On his promise to refrain from illegal activity.

Essex Man

Historical note: *The Essex coast between Southend and Rochford was ideal smuggling country, honeycombed with creeks and rivulets which became muddy tracks when the tide was out. Revenue officers were few and far between. William Blyth 'Hard Apple' lived between 1753-1830. The Blyth family is buried in Paglesham churchyard. John Harriott, a local magistrate, wrote in his memoirs many stories about Blyth which have no doubt been embellished considerably over the years.*

Captain Swing

All the protesters were long to remember
What took place on that eighth of December.
When in Little Clacton a mob did arise
That took the authorities quite by surprise.

Assembling in the dead of night
Their aim was to give their bosses a fright.
There were a lot of nefarious schemes
Involving the breaking of work machines.

The men were angry and ready to pillage
It was easy to loot and burn in their village.
With dawn breaking the riot soon got under way
Anything mechanical was smashed in the affray.

Retribution came swift and hard from the start.
No mercy was shown to anyone who took part.
Married men with children were taken away
Harsh example to those caught up in the sway.

The Captain ran, was tracked and brought down.
Incarcerated in Chelmsford gaol by the Crown.
Sentence was swift, for all to understand -
Fourteen years to be spent Van Diemen's land.

Andrew Summers

Historical Note: *In the winter of 1830/31 a great wave of protest machine breaking occurred in Southeast England. The machine breakers riot of little Clacton resulted in 50 men being convicted. The leader of the 'Swing Rioters' was a so called Captain Swing who supposedly took his name from the 'swing' or moving part of the flail used to thrash the grain. The rioters in turn were collectively referred to as Swing rioters. Nearly 2000 men and women were convicted and over 500 were transported to Van Diemen's Land (now Tasmania). In February 1835, 200 of those convicted received free pardons although most stayed on in Australia.*

Sad Days at High Beech
Alfred Lord Tennyson

Dearest Emily,
I have been here all year.
The sparkling brook is gone with a muddy pond just near.
My sleep is restless and I feel my power ebbs away,
The forest trees hem me in and keep me at bay.

I wish you were near when my light is low.
Yesterday a great thunderstorm disturbed my flow.
The critics mock me without mercy for my latest work.
I see on their faces a wicked smirk.

There are two sharp dogs that bark all night.
That disturbs me continually and adds to my plight.
This night the winds begin to rise
I fear they'll drag me further from my prize.

Dearest Emily,
I wish I could visit you.
But my means make it impossible for me to do.
I always try to cherish the things we have said.
Now I busy myself with a modern uplifting rhyme
Ever yours truly, Alfred.

Andrew Summers

Historical Note: *Alfred Lord Tennyson, wrote The Charge of the Light Brigade, The Lady of Shalot and Ulysses amongst many others. He lived in Beech Hill Park, High Beech, Epping Forest between 1837 and 1840. By all accounts it was not a happy time. Separated from his fiancée Emily Sellwood, mourning the death of a close friend and under severe financial strain, he became increasingly sensitive to criticism of his writing. During his stay in Epping his epic poem In Memoriam was started. Originally from Lincolnshire, the family moved to Tunbridge Wells in 1840. Tennyson was made Poet Laureate in 1850. Today he lies in Poets Corner, Westminster Abbey.*

Lost in Ongar

David Livingstone qualified as a doctor in Glasgow
Though he felt as a missionary his future would be.
He studied theology with Reverend Cecil in Ongar
So that he could convert heathens over the sea.

Fellow students marvelled at his energy and drive
When he walked to London and back one foggy day.
A fifty mile round trip to visit a sick relative,
And attending an accident that happened on the way.

On his return at Stanford Rivers the fog had grown thicker
He was tired and undecided which direction would be right?
Climbing the signpost to see which road would be quicker
He set off for Chipping Ongar arriving home at midnight.

When he saw David, Joseph Moore his friend said,
"He looked white as a sheet and couldn't say a word.
I gave him bread and milk and put him to bed."
Where he slept for twelve hours or more undisturbed.

Art Szmauz

Historical Note: *David Livingstone (1813-1873) was a self-educated Scot from Blantyre and trained as a doctor in Glasgow and London. Accepted as a probationer by the 'London Missionary Society', he was sent to study under the Rev. Cecil in Chipping Ongar, where for fifteen months he lodged with other students, in what are now called, 'Livingstone Cottages' in Ongar High Street. In 1840 he went to Africa where he spent the rest of his life. He travelled down the Zambezi River in 1855 to 'The smoke that thunders,' renamed in English as The Victoria Falls. The journalist Henry Morgan Stanley met him in 1871, after a long search, with the famous words, "Doctor Livingstone I presume." His 50-mile walk in Essex was a taste of things to come as he walked some 4,000 miles in Africa. David Livingstone died in Africa though his body was interred in Westminster Abbey.*

David Livingstone looking for Ongar

Christmas Day in the Workhouse

The workhouse, though much maligned,
Was paid for from the rates.
Providing basic care for the parish poor
Putting food upon their plates.

At Romford Union Workhouse then
Imagine the furore
When on Christmas day plum puddings
Were given to the poor.

The guardians were roundly castigated
The ratepayers were vexed.
Plum puddings for paupers!
On Christmas Day? What next!

Hopefully the guardians stood their ground,
Proud of 'doing good'.
And the paupers accepted their festive generosity
By enjoying the Christmas pud.

John Debenham

Historical note: *The Romford Union Workhouse was a state of the art institution when built in 1834. The Infirmary had evolved into a centre of medical knowledge by the early twentieth century and it was from this that the Oldchurch Hospital of today has grown. Part of the original buildings are now used as the Path. Lab. and a dining room. The report in the Essex Standard in 1841 quoted the 400 inmates as being given 240 plum puddings, a total weight of 600lbs.*

Hockley Spa

For London, Essex waters had become all the rage
All digestive problems they were said to assuage.
The finest mineral water containing Epson salt
Was available to all at Hockley's Spa resort.

To drink one and half pints of water was the cure
Four times a day straight from the well to be sure.
Mrs and Mrs Clay set up a business in their home,
She claiming this relieved her asthmatic syndrome.

A well was sunk, a good 10 feet deep
In anticipation of the profits they would reap.
The well never ran dry in severest drought
Or froze when coldest weather was about.

A London company saw a business opportunity
And came to invest in Hockley with some impunity.
They built a great pump room in Grecian style
Plus an upmarket hotel, hoping to make a pile.

Alas the great gamble didn't make the pass
For the waters were a fad and visitors sparse.
The railway came and Southend set the fashion.
With seawater bathing becoming a passion.

As Hockley Spa's fortunes began to decline
Viability of the business became borderline.
Sending spa water to London by cart was tried
But a pollution scare arose and the business died.

Art Szmauz

Historical Note: *The medicinal properties of Hockley's mineral waters were 'discovered' by Mr and Mrs Clay who had moved from Cheltenham in the 1830s. Both the Pump Room designed by James Lockyer and Hockley Spa Hotel were constructed in 1843. Hockley Spa water was only ever used for drinking and there were never any bathing facilities. The Spa hotel was built as an extremely grand hotel for its time, it is now a public house. The pump room has since been incorporated into an adjacent building but the façade still remains.*

The Coggeshall Gang

'The Coggeshall Gang', as they came to be known
Were a blot on the history of that peaceable town.
In the Eighteen-forties criminal activities were rife,
Thefts, arson, assault; causing all manner of strife.

On a house in Coggeshall their reign of terror began,
To rob Charles Skingsley was their dastardly plan.
Mr Skingsley was away on the night they broke in
So they burnt down his house and stole all his wine.

'The Bird in Hand' public house suffered burglary
Followed by the plundering of Richard Bell's grocery.
William French, the landlord of the Black Horse Inn
Was the 'fence', receiving the swag they brought in.

The gang entered James Finch's house one night.
Over the fire they near set his housekeeper alight,
Strung James up to a beam with a rope round his neck,
Torturing both to reveal where their money was kept.

In 1847 one gang member, William Wade was arrested.
Turning Queens Evidence, the others names he attested.
Despite efforts to flee the gang were all apprehended
And Coggeshall could relax the reign of terror was ended.

At their trial, found guilty, the judge took a firm stand
Saying all would be transported to Van Diemen's Land.
A life sentence for three, the rest seven years were given
Crow, their leader did not go with them; he died in prison.

John Debenham

Historical note: *The Essex Constabulary was only formed in 1840. The apprehending of the Coggeshall Gang was an early test of their resolve and determination. The gang terrorised the Coggeshall area, the height of their activities being 1844 - 1848. Wade was arrested and imprisoned. Samuel Crow, the gang leader, visiting him in 1848 promised to look after his wife in exchange for his silence. When this help failed to materialise Wade turned Queen's evidence giving the names of the gang to the governor of Chelmsford prison. The gang fled some taking ship for America, some for Hamburg, some hiding locally. All were caught by the Constabulary within the year.*

LAUNCH OF THE WARRIOR

It was the coldest winter for 50 years,
Braziers blazed as completion neared.
Frozen snow covered the yard and river Thames,
And dockside cranes sparkled as if decked in gems.

Two thousand frenzied workers laboured day and night,
Watched by crowds well wrapped 'gainst winter's chilling bite.
The ship's vast hull rose tall in its cocoon of scaffold
Like a monolithic iron skyscraper breaking the mould.

The day of the launch came, but there was a glitch.
It was stuck to the slipway on its icy pitch.
Hundreds of men on deck tried to rock her loose,
Whilst tugs dragged to free her from the icy noose.

After 20 minutes, the 'Warrior' finally gave way
And the ship dropped from its launch bay.
The First Lord smashed a bottle of wine over her bow.
"God speed the 'Warrior' - your time is now"

Andrew Summers

Historical Note: *The Thames Ironworks was the most important shipbuilding works on the River Thames in 1860. Over 900 vessels had been launched from its Bow Creek shipyard. HMS Warrior was Britain's first iron-hulled warship and launched on December 29th 1860. The vessel never fired a shot in anger and within 10 years was obsolete. The Warrior has since been restored and serves as a museum ship at Portsmouth. Thames Ironworks closed in 1912. The only memory of the company is in the badge and nickname of its works football team, West Ham United FC. 'Ironworks' long ago became shortened to 'Irons' and 'Hammers' refers not to 'West Ham' but to the crossed tools on the club badge.*

Thames Barge

Out there she lies, sedately on the tide,
A legacy of dim-departed seas –
The block across the horse begins to slide
As fill the sails aslant the western breeze.

An evening fades to ochre on the ebb
As down the dredge she drifts toward the east –
She rides the waves, a bluff and blunted head,
Across the shoals to far-forgotten quays.

And we are there, our memories abaft,
To haul the sheet and leave the land behind –
To tack upon the swatchways of our past
Beyond the shallowing moorings of the mind.

Yes, we were there, a sheer above the silt,
A ripple on the passage of our days –
Our wake is cut beneath the spirit's keel
And every moon diminished by its phase.

Mervyn Linford

Historical Note: *Records suggest that the first Essex sailing barge was built in in Rettendon in 1791 and the last built in 1928 in Mistley. In their heyday, the 1860s, over 5000 barges plied their trade along the East Coast between Kent and Essex. Today about 25 are left in sailing condition based around Maldon. Most are used for sail charter and training. Swatchway: a navigable channel at low tide.*

Onward, Christian Soldiers

"Onward, Christian soldiers, marching as to war,
With the cross of Jesus going on before."
The opening lines of the immortal hymn
Written by the Rector of East Mersea on a whim.

Reverend Sabine Baring-Gould had decided to write
A hymn and was willed to complete it overnight.
He mused; the rhymes were faulty and not well based.
He freely admitted – the result of penning in haste.

It was composed for children to sing with body and soul
When walking along together for a common goal.
The hymn immediately became a great success
Much to the surprise of the Rector as he would confess.

Andrew Summers

Historical Note: *The Reverend Sabine Baring-Gould, was the Rector at East Mersea Church of St Edmunds from 1871 to 1881. 'Onward, Christian Soldiers' was written in 1865 with music by Arthur Sullivan. The author wrote several books including 'Mehalah' published in 1880 set in and around Mersea Island. East Mersea Church was built in 13th Century in the reign of King John. The hymn was sung at the funeral of American president Dwight Eisenhower at the National Cathedral, Washington DC, in March 1969.*

The Sea Witch

The Sea Witch, she was known as in Leigh,
Living in a cottage off Victoria Wharf.
Hare lipped and hook nosed
Sarah Moore was the stuff of witch legend.

She foretold the sex of the unborn child
And could say what the future would hold.
To upset her would risk a terrible curse
That might last for generations to come.

A sailor refusing to 'Buy a fair wind',
Was no sooner afloat than capsized.
Sparks from her eyes caught children on fire,
She put curses on others that soon died.

The legends, with the benefit of study and research,
Can mostly be explained away through
Outbreaks of cholera and child killing diseases,
Accidents with candles and paraffin lamps.

Yet to upset 'Mother Moore' was not done lightly.
Feared till she died, her memory in legend secure.
She's remembered in time honoured fashion
In Leigh, with a pub named 'The Sarah Moore'.

John Debenham

Historical Note: *Sarah Moore was known as The Sea Witch and lived in Leigh until her death in 1867. This is a matter of record as are affirmations, and explanations, of some of the legends. There are family connections today,with some of these legends recorded by Sheila Pitt-Stanley in her book 'Legends Of Leigh'. The pub 'The Sarah Moore', in Elm Road Leigh, part of the Wizard Inns Chain, was established in 1998 and named to reflect this legend of Old Leigh and the chain's policy of 'Locals for Locals'.*

Southend Watch Vessel No 7

Watch Vessel Number Seven, no more to function.
Sold for salvage, destined for destruction.
Abandoned on the banks of the River Roach
Now lies deep in the mud of Pagelsham Reach.

The vessel's last duty was as a static base
For government officials to guard and chase
Oyster thieves and nefarious persons
That came at night on illegal excursions.

This ship had sailed the whole world round.
Charting the coasts of the Lands that were found.
The venture's success, the most famous of many
Has become embedded in the nation's history.

Charles Darwin; ship's naturalist, observed and recorded
In Galapagos islands how the life chain was ordered.
His observations he later worked into a thesis,
And published controversially in 'Origin of Species'.

Despite the ship's exotic and illustrious career
No museum or dignified resting-place was near.
This abandoned hulk in the mud; so unregal,
Yet many will remember, 'The Voyage of The Beagle'.

John Debenham

Historical note: *HMS Beagle was originally launched as one of 15 Cherokee-class, 10 gun Brigs. Built for the Royal Navy in 1807, it was used in a variety of roles including Surveying and Anti-slavery patrols. The Beagle was recently discovered as a result of research for the naming of the Beagle II space capsule in 2004. 'The Beagle' is best remembered for its epic 5 year voyage of 1831, charting the coasts of Patagonia and Tierra del Fuego, in which Darwin, as the expedition naturalist, made the observations which led to his theories of evolution, published as 'The Origin Of Species', in 1859.*

Coalhouse Fort

Not a pretty building, this.
Thick stone walls concealing dank
And dingy corridors, and rooms
As dark as caves where once the spite
Of gunpowder and shells was stacked.

Above them, casements, where the huge
Front loaded guns were fed and fired
By men who polished them with love,
Though wary of their violence,
And slept beside them in their cage.

Eyes were trained across the bank
Of earth that could contain a blast,
Scanning down the River Thames
For foreign sails, an enemy fleet
Maybe coming into view.

But there were none. The big black guns
Were tried and tested in thin air,
But not a shot was fired in war
To deafen birds and animals
That shared this leafy site.

Not a pretty building this.
Obsolete the walls become
A backdrop to a Batman film
As children climb on playground swings,
Play football on the grass.

Katie Mallett

Historical Note: *Coalhouse Fort, East Tilbury was completed in 1874, under the Supervision of Colonel, later General, Charles Gordon (of Khartoum fame) and was one the Palmerston Forts. These forts were built to guard against the perceived threat of continental invasion, yet were never called into action. Since 1983 the Fort has been leased to the Coalhouse Fort Project as a visitor attraction.*

The Lopper of Loughton

Lopping was granted by ancient right,
Not to be surrendered without a fight,
To commoners gathering wood as fuel
When winter nights were cold and cruel.

On Mondays from 1st November to April
Woodcutters would gather on Staples Hill.
As commoners had done since Tudor times
To stock up with fuel 'gainst winter climes.

William Maitland, Lord of the Manor, had planned
To enclose the forest, get the loppers banned,
Then harvest the wood and profit much more.
By selling it on - technically breaking the law.

Secretly supported by the Forest Commission
Maitland was helped get judicial permission.
When he invited all the loppers to the King's Head
Thomas Willingale saw they were being misled,

Like Maitland he knew that the loppers rights
Would be forfeit if not exercised by midnight.
He waited and just before the midnight chime
Ran to the forest to lop branches, just in time.

Essex Man

***Historical Note:** "Lopping" was the ancient practice of cutting or lopping the branches of trees by commoners in Epping Forest for use as fuel during winter. Thomas Willingale a woodcutter from Loughton firmly believed that if no one started lopping at the appointed hour, the rights, which applied from 1st November to 23rd April, would be lost forever. In the 1860s the Lords of the Manor lead by William Maitland gradually fenced off more and more of Epping Forest and were keen to stop the established lopping rights. In 1878 the Corporation of London took control of management of the Forest as an open space for public recreation. All illegally enclosed lands, except those actually built on were opened. The City of London paid £7,000 for the extinction of the lopping rights and with this money the Lopping Hall in Loughton was built.*

William Morris

His colours reflect the landscape,
Of Essex rolling downs.
Each thread or blade of grass
And stitch of golden corn.

A fleur-de-lis of emblems
From local village signs,
Line his flowering drapes
And cover grand walls.

Each word is an art form
In poems and script.
Retaining Victorian splendour
For a concrete age.

He shared his craft with others
Creating the Kelmscott style,
Unique but very English
Renowned throughout the world.

Christine Billington

Historical Note: *William Morris was one of the principal founders of the British Arts and Crafts Movement and is best known as a designer of wallpaper and patterned fabrics, a writer of poetry and fiction, and an early founder of the socialist movement in Britain. He was born in Walthamstow in 1834, and spent his early years in what was then rural Essex which left a profound and lasting impression on him. In a letter in 1883 he described Walthamstow 'as a suburban village on the edge of Epping Forest, and once a pleasant place enough, but now terribly cocknified and choked up by the jerry-builder ' At the age of 14 Morris moved from Woodford Hall to Water House which has since become the William Morris Gallery.*

Earthquake

Nine twenty a.m. on a bright Tuesday morning
Peldon and Abberton, Wivenhoe way,
Sunny the sky, as it came without warning,
The rumbling, the thunder below on that day.

Underground movements are rare to this nation,
Earthquakes are something just few of us see.
Shaken and stirred was an awed population
Storm-tossed like boats on an earth-coloured sea.

In less than a minute some twelve hundred buildings
Were damaged or shattered by waves in the round.
Churches lost battlements. Towers and spires,
Broken and rent, tumbled down to the ground.

Chimneys came smashing through roofs they'd surmounted,
Walls cracked and masonry clattered about.
People ran outdoors, confused and haunted.
Earth rose and fell as the shockwaves spread out.

Farmer and horses in fields shook and stumbled.
Little Wigb'rough's tower lost many a tier.
Fissures on Mersea. The Peldon mill tumbled.
At Southend a fisherman fell off the pier.

Robert Hallmann

Historical Note: *'A low rumbling proceeding from the earth, not from above; a rolling sound, indescribable, unlike anything else' was how one eyewitness described it. On 22 April 1884, the largest earthquake in this country's memory was centred close to Colchester, under the farming communities of Peldon, Abberton and Wivenhoe. In less than a minute some 1200 buildings, cottages, mansions, churches and business premises were damaged or shattered in a 150 mile radius. Hundreds were made homeless, though people survived remarkably well.*

Tiptree Jam

'By their fruits shall ye know them'

Strawberries, raspberries, gooseberries and cherries;
Currants, damsons, quinces and plums
Glorious fruit all there for the picking
At Tiptree - the land of superior jams.

The good Arthur Wilkin was going to market
His horse-drawn cart fair laden with fruit
At Kelvedon station he watched the rough loading
And thought of the perils it faced while on route.

He asked his wife for her jam recipes
And learned how to make them
With much expertise
Then he founded his factory
Famous for jam.

As the company flourished
He changed the old name
From Britannia to Wilkin
And thus grew its fame.

From small beginnings
He made Jam galore
Praised by the famous
Like Gladstone and more.

To this present day enjoyed by us all
With new flavours to tempt us
And hold us in thrall.

Shirley Baker

Historical Note: *Wilkin and Sons Limited have been making the world famous Tiptree preserves in the village of Tiptree for more than 115 years. Founded in 1885 by A. C. Wilkin it is still a privately owned family business. Farming approximately 1,000 acres in and around Tiptree it employs nearly 200 people. Holding royal warrants for both preserves and marmalades Wilkin supplies most UK fine food shops and major supermarket groups and exports to more than sixty countries world-wide. Visitors are always welcome at the Tiptree Tea Room where the range of products may be sampled, with homemade scones and cream, Monday to Saturday every week, except over the Christmas period.*

Give Us Back Our Essex

Bishops Stortford's Poor Law Union Board
Had villages in Essex and Herts to care for.
Paying the least they were forced to afford
Barely keeping the poorest from death's door.

The Guardians, to keep Workhouse rates down
Thought of wheezes to curb administration.
'Take the Essex villages, make them our own',
Was one Hertfordshire biased solution?

In 1888 the national boundary commission,
Finding a kink in county borders on their charts,
Decided in order to correct this remission
Ten Essex villages would be taken into Herts.

A proposal was made to straighten the border.
Poor-law Guardians thought costs would deflate.
Cried the villagers, inflamed in riotous disorder,
'We've been Essex Men since Alfred the Great.'

Five villages; Manewdon, Farnham, Elsenham,
And Stansted, home of the Mountfitchet clan,
Together with Ugley, vowed to the last man
To defeat this bureaucratic, opportunist plan.

Led by Fuller-Maitland, who rebuilt Stansted Hall
The plan was defeated the county line preserved.
All the Essex villages stayed, ten of them in all,
Their loyalty rewarded, their victory deserved.

John Debenham

Historical note: *After the Poor Law Amendment Act of 1834, Bishops Stortford Poor Law Union was formed. In 1888 to reduce costs the Board of Guardians colluded with the Boundaries Commission, in what for them was a tidying up, to transfer five villages from Essex to Hertfordshire. One of the leaders of the considerable opposition to this plan, William Fuller-Maitland, was responsible for the rebuilding of Stansted Hall where his family lived until 1921.*

Kynochtown

In 1890 from Birmingham the firm of Messrs Kynoch
Came to Thames Haven where their ships could dock.
They had a wide ranging armaments business to extend
Including smokeless powder at the lower end.

To support the new factory a new town was born
With houses, a shop, a club and a brand new lawn.
There was a school, a cricket and a football team
And a new hotel on Canvey, just across the stream.

With the start of the Great War, a hospital came
And a fire and police station to great acclaim.
But the factory was subject to floods from the river
And danger from bombs that aircraft could now deliver

1919 cutbacks closed the factory and oil became the theme.
Cory Brothers from Cardiff were the new owners on the scene.
Kynochtown was renamed as old patrons had gone,
And the new site for oil refining was renamed Coryton.

Andrew Summers

Historical Note: *In 1950 The Vacuum Oil Company (later Mobil Oil) took over the site from Cory Brothers and built their own oil refinery. In 1953 the town was flooded and all residents evacuated. Unlike Canvey Island there was no loss of life. In 1969 the Mobil Oil Company expanded the refinery again, leaving Coryton Village located in the middle of a giant industrial complex. In the interests of safety all the remaining villagers were re-housed and by 1974 the Village had been completely demolished.*

Longer than a Mile

Oh Southend Pier longer than a mile!
I'm treading your boards walking in style.
What does the future hold my old friend?
What will I find when I get to the end?

Southend Pier, you watch us all pass by
And on my walk I stop and wonder why.
Bold schemes for your future come and go
Whilst you remain passive in the Thames' flow.

And what ill luck has come your way
Will the jinx of fire be lifted some day?
And a vessel, off course slicing you in two
Must have felt like a dagger running you through.

Oh Southend Pier you make us smile
You give us pleasure once in a while.
Yet solid and calm in the mud you stand
A pier above piers in a dwindling band.

At the end I see Kent from your pier head,
Ships up close and the lifeboat in its shed,
Oh! Southend Pier longer than a mile
I'm on your train riding back in style.

Andrew Summers

Historical Note: *Southend's first wooden pier was opened in 1830. Extended in 1846 it was the longest in Europe at nearly 7,000 feet. It was replaced by the Iron Pier, complete with electric railway, in 1890.*

William Bradley, born in 1850, was the first full-time Pier-Head Man in 1871. He was rewarded for his lifesaving bravery by the Royal Humane Society as well as the Council and was actively involved in the formation of the RNLI in Southend. Today's Pier has survived numerous boat crashes; two world wars; being requisitioned as 'HMS Leigh' by the Navy, and four major fires. After the most recent fire in October 2005 the council stated that the pier will be restored. It is still, at 1.34 miles (2158M) the longest pleasure pier in the world.

Salvation Army Colony.

The Salvation Army bought the land
High above the Old Leigh strand.
The unemployed from London towns
Were brought by Booth to Hadleigh Downs,
To his new farm colony to learn a trade:
Save their souls? Have a new life made?

Down Castle Lane they built their farm
With accommodation to house the swarm
Of colonists that herded cows and sheep
Or laboured in the fields to earn their keep.

The Hadleigh villagers were opposed at first;
Destitute vagabonds! They feared the worst,
Fighting and thieving, stock would be lost.
The colony would close off paths that crossed
Their land, denying access to the nicer parts
Where locals picked berries for pies and tarts.

The plan developed; village fears came to nought.
Other trades as well as farming were taught:
Brickmaking, pottery and construction skills
Were learned by many on the riverside hills.

Today training continues in a number of ways
Farm produce is sold on monthly market days.
There is a rare breeds centre with visitor information
And a trainee run tea-room with a growing reputation.

Dominating the view the castle ruins stand bare
The colonists long gone but 'The Army' is still there.

Essex Man

Inspired by John Barr's poem in Darkest England

Historical Notes: *In his 1890 book 'In Darkest England and the Way Out', General William Booth outlined proposals to help the thousands of destitute unemployed of London. In 1891 he founded the 'Salvation Army Farm Colony' on the Thames estuary at Hadleigh in Essex. Eventually 3,200 acres the estate encompassed the Castle, and Park and Sayers farms to the south of Hadleigh Village. There was opposition from Hadleigh residents at the prospect of London's poor and destitute descending on them. A Local paper accused General Booth of acting as the 'Baron of Hadleigh'. The Salvation Army transformed the neglected farms and by the end of 1891 over 200 'colonists' were on site. Along with farming and market gardening they were taught brick making, pottery and construction skills in the estate's own works. By its 21st anniversary the Army had trained some 7,000 colonists. In the 1960s the farms were running on a commercial basis with profits going to general Salvation Army funds. The 1990s brought strengthened links with the local community and new training opportunities. These include a Rare Breeds Centre, Tea Rooms and the Home Farm Nursery whose organic fruit and vegetables are sold to the local community. There is also a monthly Farmers' Market, run jointly by the training centre and the farm.*

The Gilbey Accolade,
The Prettiest Village in England

The 'Rambler' newspaper didn't last.
With insufficient support it faded fast
It soon disappeared without much ado,
Some weeks after making a splashy debut.

Within its columns appeared a request,
Putting readers' observation to the test,
To nominate the prettiest village in the land.
Replies please; written in your own hand.

Many replies came in and a result was achieved
From Sir Walter Gilbey this reply was received.
A man of the utmost propriety, he wrote with the authority
Of President no less, of the Royal Agricultural Society.

"Sir, in reply to your request, if you ask me,
The prettiest village in the East, well let me see,
I would say Finchingfield, beyond that I cannot go,
Having considered this in depth, it is so".

Essex Man

Historical Note: *Thus 'Gilbey's Accolade' was born in 'The Rambler' of 12th February 1898. The terse words took on a life of their own.*
Although a short lived publication, the words were picked up by the Essex County Chronicle and then repeated often by numerous publications over the next 100 years. Many painters have been inspired by the village including Lucien Pissarro and Alfred Munnings. It is said that Munnings was more interested in the ladies attending the art classes than art or the village itself. Finchingfield now earns the name of the most photographed village in England.

Timeline

Essex Event Commemorated	Year	National or International Event
Courtaulds gets rights to 'Viscose'	1904	*Panama Canal started*
Arthur Joscelyne Snr. leases Joselyn's beach Chalkwell	1909	*Louis Bleriot first to fly the English Channel*
Morris Dancing Starts in Thaxted	1911	*Hiram Bingham finds Machu Picchu*
Death of Captain Oats	1912	*Titanic sinks on maiden voyage*
Zeppelin L33 crashes at Lt Wigborough	1916	*Battle of the Somme*
Kynocktown becomes Coryton	1919	*IRA is formed*
Loftus Arkwright disappears	1919	*League of Nations founded in Paris*
First Public Entertainment Broadcast	1920	*Prohibition comes into effect in USA*
Bertram the Clown opens in Clacton	1922	*Stalin becomes Soviet Leader*
Crittals Model Village created	1925	*Logie Baird transmits TV pictures*
Borley Rectory Investigated	1928	*Fleming discovers Penicillin*
Happy Harry assaulted in Southend	1929	*Debut of Popeye in comic strip*
Two Churches in Willingale combine	1929	*Wall Street Crash*
Plotlanders expansion in Dunton	1930	*First Football World Cup*
Ford begins production in Dagenham	1931	*National Government formed in UK*
Bata Shoe Factory opens East Tilbury	1933	*Hitler appointed German Chancellor*
Galleywood Racecourse closed	1935	*Alcoholics Anonymous formed in NY*
	1939	*Start of World War II*
Leigh boats rescue troops from Dunkirk	1940	*Winston Churchill becomes PM*
RAF Bradwell Bay opens	1942	*Irving Berlin writes White Christmas*
Stansted Airport opens as USAF base	1943	*Battle of Stalingrad ends*
Mulberry Harbour Section sinks in Thames Estuary	1944	*'D Day' Landings in Normandy*
	1945	*World War II Ends*
The Great Surge: Essex Floods	1953	*Hilary and Tensing climb Mt Everest*
Bradwell Nuclear Power Station opens	1962	*Uganda becomes independent*
Last train from Saffron Walden	1964	*BBC2 starts broadcasting*
Radio Caroline begins broadcasting	1964	*Harold Wilson becomes PM*
GLC formed Essex borders changed	1965	*Rhodesia declares UDI*
Radio Caroline silenced by storms	1966	*England Wins World Cup*
Weely Rock Festival	1971	*Decimal currency introduced in UK*
Chelmer Navigation closed to freight	1972	*Bloody Sunday in Northern Ireland*
Southend Pier Head destroyed by fire	1976	*First Concorde passenger flight*
Space Shuttle Enterprise lands at Stansted	1983	*Margaret Thatcher wins 2nd Election*
New Terminal opened at Stansted	1991	*First Gulf War, Iraq invades Kuwait*
Nuclear Bunker Decommissioned	1992	*'Black Wednesday' UK leaves ERM*
Elizabeth Fry new face of £5.00 note	1992	*English FA Premier League formed*
Brightlingsea Live Animal export protests	1995	*OJ Simpson verdict: 'Not guilty'*
Death of Sir Alf Ramsay	1999	*Welsh Assembly opens in Cardiff*
Bradwell Nuclear Power Station Closes	2002	*EURO notes and coins introduced.*

Family Courtauld

George Courtauld - descendant of a French refugee
Opened a silk mill in the town of Braintree.
After nine good years he retired knowing well
That the mill would be safe with son Samuel.

Sam expanded the business to Halstead and Bocking
Investing in steam power which some thought shocking.
When they went on strike he gave the leaders the sack
For their impertinence. The rest all came back.

Courtaulds were very fair as major employers,
Strong on welfare they looked after there workers.
The first company in England to employ a nurse,
Sam's wife ran a créche for children, also a first.

The workers were unique when, in a great celebration
To honour their employers they formed in procession.
They marched with silk banners to a marquee in the town,
Where sixteen hundred of the company all could sit down.

The procession was over a mile in length
Seven thousand spectators attended the event.
With dinner and speeches over and banners presented
The day ended with fireworks and all went home contented.

The Courtauld legacy may still be seen by visitors to Braintree.
The museum, once 'Manor Street School' was given in 1863.
'The Braintree and Bocking Institute' for study and inspiration;
The Public Gardens, The Town Hall (now tourist information).

These are some of the monuments to the family that live on
But the factories that made their wealth are now long gone.

John Debenham

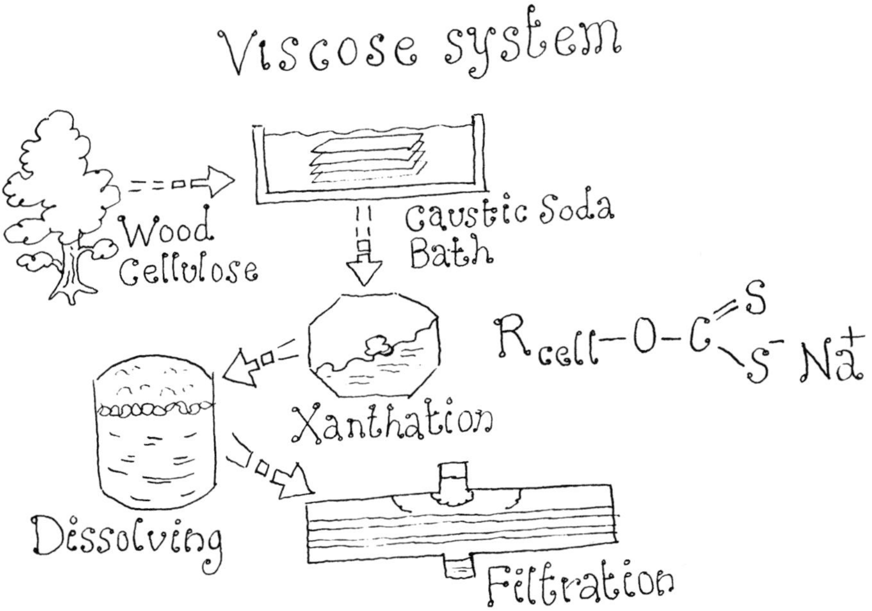

Viscose system

Wood Cellulose

Caustic Soda Bath

$R_{cell}-O-C(=S)-S^{-}\,Na^{+}$

Xanthation

Dissolving

Filtration

Historical Note: *Though Samuel Courtauld II put the company on the road to success it was always a family concern. Brothers, cousins, sons all played their part. Courtaulds started to become the world wide organisation it is today when in 1904 the rights to the 'viscose system' were acquired. This led to the discovery of 'Rayon' and many other 'man-made' materials revolutionising the clothing industry as well as products as diverse as tyres, transmission belts, furnishing fabrics and even cigarette filters. Samuel IV the chairman until 1946, together with Viscount Lee of Farnham and Sir Robert Witt, were responsible for the foundation of 'The Courtauld Institute' which continues the family tradition of always putting something back into society.*

JOSCELYNE'S BEACH CHALKWELL
(AN EDWARDIAN MELODRAMA)

"Nine pound". She cried, "Nine pound!
To lease a stretch of shingle;
Stony sand and ground left over from the MRC.
Eight mouths to feed and a baby at my breast.
Our money gone in just one thoughtless act.
By a drunken sot who lost the
lot in an auction at the Smack".

Impetuous, hot headed, resourceful to the last
He wheeled and dealed and gave his name
To that section of the shore - hired tents and skiffs
And fishing trips and costumes to the poorest folk
Who visited on summer days to take their ease
At Chalkwell Bay in times before the War.

That Beach became the death of him so Minnie took it over;
Her tender heart became as stone with the loss of her wild lover.
Stately and cool she ruled her patch - Ma Joscelyne was a queen.
The children helped and did their bit and her dynasty remained
Full forty years 'til the lease was taken from her hand
And the LTS took over - both livelihood and land.

Clare Harvey

***Historical Note:** In 1909 Arthur Joscelyne Snr. purchased the lease on a beach behind Chalkwell station in a drunken moment. Somehow he made a business out of it. In 1917 he was clearing up after a great storm when a strangulated hernia resulted in his sudden death. Everyone said Ellen Elizabeth (Minnie) his wife could not carry on because women just did not run businesses. With the help of her eldest son Arthur Jnr. (Sonny) and the younger children, she became somewhat of a martinet and ran it until 1949.*

THAXTED

In twelve-eighty-seven one Richard de Taxte
Was known as a hafter in the village of Thaxted.
In thirteen-ninety the Guildhall was built
By the Guild of the Cutlers who made knife, axe and hilt
And halberds and surgeons' tools of renown,
When Stoney Road still was the main road in town.
Upon the old cobbles tradition fared well
And harmony, music and dance cast their spell.
The Morris Ring formed here in nineteen eleven,
Since then the towns been the Morris Men's heaven.
The organ was played by a Maestro magician,
Whose music took wings over craft and tradition.
He soared to 'The Planets', we listen entranced...
A blue plaque marks mortar this genius enhanced.
'Gustav Holst', Composer', a master of sound.
His house and its garden were fertile ground.
A 'Choral Symphony' grew among flowers,
A 'Festival Chorus' – his music is ours:-
'Our Church-bells in Thaxted at Whitsuntide say,
Come all you good people and put care away...'

Robert Hallmann

Historical Note: *Vicar Conrad Noel started Morris dancing in Thaxted in 1911 – The Thaxted Morris Men. The town has hosted a gathering of Morris dancers every year since 1927. The Ring was constituted in June 1934. The composer Gustav Holst lived for many years in Thaxted, first in Monk Street Cottages, and then from 1917 to 1925 in the Manse on Town Street. Whilst in Thaxted he composed at least part of the famous suites 'The Planets', 'Choral Symphony' and 'Tomorrow shall be my dancing day'. His Festival Chorus 'Our Church- Bells in Thaxted' was one of the works he wrote specially for the town.*

I May Be Some Time.

Known sometime as 'Titus' or 'Soldier'
Captain Oates, a well known explorer,
Was invited by Scott join his expedition,
To reach the South Pole before Amundsen.

A hand picked team of five reached the target
To find the Norwegians had beaten them to it.
Amundsen's dogs were faster, didn't get stuck.
Scott's return, on foot, was dogged with bad luck.

"I'm just going outside and may be some time."
Simple words, profoundly spoken to chime
With thoughts of colleagues who understood
Oates' ultimate sacrifice to lighten their load.

Whatever his feelings, stepping out of the tent,
Frostbitten and gangrenous, his life was spent.
Knowing that with him they could not survive
He was giving them a chance of staying alive.

Gestingthorpe has conserved the memory
Of this famous son of the Oates family
And a visitor to this North Essex village
Will see on the village sign, Captain Oates visage.

John Debenham

Historical note: *Captain L.E.G.Oates, was one of five, led by Robert Falcon Scott, who made it to the South Pole in 1912. He died, as did, despite his sacrifice, all the others on the ill fated return journey.*

L33

Having dropped bombs on London without inhibition
The Zeppelin turned for home to complete its mission
Then gunners scored a hit and night fighters attacked,
L33, was fatally wounded and wouldn't make it back.

Limping over Mersea fast losing height,
Captain Bocker feared that the end was in sight.
In the sea he knew they would come to most harm
So crash-landed in a field on a Little Wigborough farm.

The crew survived and were quickly deployed
Setting fire to their vessel - it had to be destroyed.
As the Zeppelin burned they thought what to do.
Surrender was chosen; their options were few.

Locals came out to investigate
What lit up the sky on the farm estate.
PC Nicholas cycled up to see what was aflame,
Asked Bocker and his crew if they were to blame?

Arresting them all they marched in formation.
To Peldon post office, there was no police station.
There the army were called to take charge of the men
This Zeppelin crew would not fly again.

John Debenham

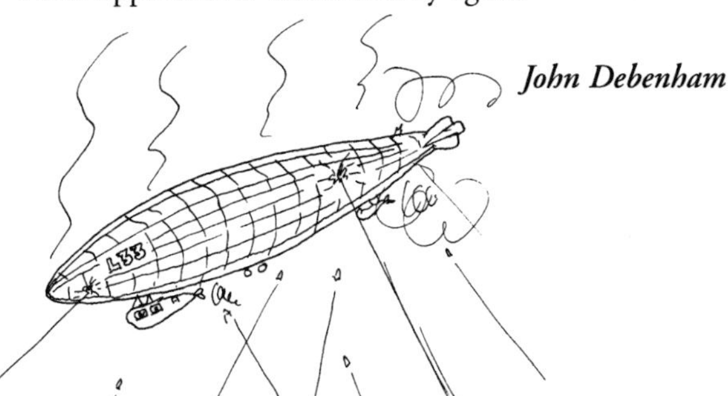

Historical Note: *In September 1916 German super airships attacked London. Each carried two million cubic feet of gas in an impregnated varnished envelope over a framework of strengthened aluminium, 680 feet long. The L33, under Kapitänleutnant Alois Böcker, had been hit by aircraft fire and lost altitude to such a degree that it turned back and crash-landed near Little Wigborough. The crew burnt the Zeppelin before marching off to surrender. The companion ship, L22, was shot down over Billericay and all the crew were killed.*

MISSING PERSON FROM HARLOW.

Do you know the whereabouts of this man?

Old Loftus Arkwright was never the same
When his son went missing - of the same name.
He was due to inherit the family estates
But worked in a garage - no interest in traits.

Sir Richard his ancestor famous for mills,
Spinning cotton for profit with no time for ills,
Wealthy landowners and Reverends to boot,
Young Loftus Arkwright did not care one hoot!

So he left and all the surmises began
Did he emigrate or wander without any plan?
He went from fair Harlow we do not know where,
'Disappeared' on his family tree - if you look for him there.

But he must have gone somewhere
Why? Was he well?
If you know the answer
Come forward - and tell!

Shirley Baker

Historical Note: *Richard Arkwright patented a cotton spinning machine in 1769. The Arkwright 'waterframe became a pillar of the industrial revolution which in turn made him a fortune. Loftus Arkwright was the great grandson of the Rev Joseph Arkwright the first Arkwright to acquire land in Harlow in 1818 (including Mark Hall where Queen Elizabeth I stayed.) Loftus was born in 1895 followed in 1901 by his twin brothers Godfrey and John. John was killed during the Second World War and Godfrey died in 1954. What happened to Loftus is a complete mystery. He would have been 25 at the time he went missing in 1919. The Arkwright estates in Harlow have all since been sold off either as railway land or to the Harlow Development corporation. John Arkwright (born 1931) is a patron of St. Mary-at Latton church although he now lives abroad.*

Radio 2MT (TwoEmmaToc)

The inventor of radio and wireless
His genius unrecognized in Rome.
Marconi came to England seeking success
And made Chelmsford his technical home.

A factory in Hall Street he took in hand,
The building stands there to this day.
His business grew and such the demand
A new factory in Writtle was soon under way.

He developed a system of sound transmission,
For its ultimate test a concert was planned.
From a studio in New Street on the 15th of June
Call sign 2MT was first heard across the land.

Throughout his experimental broadcasting
Mass communication was his holy grail.
And Dame Nellie Melba was invited to sing
With sponsorship from The Daily Mail.

The success of the event was plain to see
Later the BBC's 2LO was formed.
But broadcasting on call sign 2MT
Chelmsford was where radio was born.

John Debenham

Historical Note: *Guglielmo Marconi discovered radio in 1895. Spurned by the Italian government, he came to England and set up, in 1898, 'The Wireless Telegraph and Signal Co, Ltd' in an old silk factory in Hall Street Chelmsford. The growth of radio led to the New Street factory being built in Writtle, Chelmsford. It was from here in a makeshift studio in 1920 that dame Nellie Melba made the first advertised, Public Entertainment Broadcast, in the world. From these beginnings the Marconi Company became one of the giants of the world of communications.*

Dame Nellie Melba

Bertram the Clown

'Good morning Sir,' said the shy young fan
Ernest Kingsman barked 'I'm a very busy man.'
'Would be obliged Sir, if you'd give me a trial.'
'Come at three, don't be late and I'll see if I like your style.'

At three Clown Bertram performed and impressed the boss.
Then for 15 years the pier never made a loss.
Clown Bertram with the 'Bright Young Things' wowed the crowd.
The children shrieked with laughter and cried out loud.

Andrew Summers

Historical Note: *Clown Bertram performed on Clacton Pier every summer season from 1922 until 1939. The show was so popular a Children's Theatre was specially built for it. Originally accommodating 500, capacity was soon increased to 1000 and the show moved to the Pier Pavilion. Clacton Pier was opened in 1887. Its original use was as a landing stage for Woolwich Steam Company Packet Steamers.*

'New Jerusalem'

Crittall's Braintree factory was at maximum capacity.
Expansion was needed to meet growing demand.
Workers could be hired but with nowhere to house them,
What was a keen socialist like Francis Crittall to do?

Titus Salt, George Cadbury, Ebenezer Howard;
Francis Crittall had admired them all.
He reflected on their common principle
Of putting people at the centre of the plan.

He would build his 'New Jerusalem' in rural Silver End.
A vision developed of houses in tree-lined streets,
A factory that was 'state of the art', where workers
Wouldn't be 'grist to the mill' but able to play a full part.

The village was built, Crittall's vision stayed true.
Each house and its garden on wide tree lined streets,
Had hot and cold running water and electricity laid
In unlimited supply from the new factory's plant.

Church, school and shops, a cinema too,
An independent drainage system,
The farm growing food to be bought at the store,
Made the village very much self-sufficient.

With workers housed and happy with their lot
Crittall's business grew and blossomed.
Frances with his wife lived the rest of his life
In 'The Manors' in the village he created.

John Debenham

Historical note: *Crittall Standardized Steel Windows revolutionised the building industry in the 1920s. At Bears Tye Farm, in 1925 the model village of Silver End was created. Built by Crittalls to house workers for the new factory. It was self sufficient with school, Church and shops. In 1927 the school had a roll of 135 pupils. The village was built by Crittall's 'Silver End Development Company'. Taken over by Slater Walker Securities in 1968 the houses were acquired by Witham Council, though many are now privately owned the village is a designated conservation area.*
Titus Salt built 'Saltaire' and George Cadbury, 'Bournville' villages for their workers. Ebenezer Howard was the founder of the garden City Movement responsible, in 1903, for Letchworth Garden City.

Haunted House

Borley Rectory sadly is no more.
A lamp was knocked over on a pile of books
And the days, and nights, of yore
Were gone (or were they?) for the resident spooks.

Once reputed the most haunted house in England
With strange goings on and weird sightings
Like the black clothed Nun seen walking her path
Or a horse drawn coach with a headless man driving.

The Rectory was built; it is said, on an old monastic site
With French Nuns living in a Priory near by.
Long ago a Monk eloped with a Nun from there,
The authorities then raised a hue and cry.

They were caught and brought back, so the tale goes.
He was executed. She was bricked up in her convent.
But true love never dies and their spirits lived on
To roam for eternity, their state to lament.

In the Rectory of late there's been quite a 'to do'
Unseen hands would write messages on the wall,
Books appear and disappear in the smallest room
And objects from shelves would unaccountably fall.

In the nineteen thirties the Daily Mirror got to hear
Of happenings that defied explanation.
A reporter and psychical researcher were sent
To investigate, and explain to the nation.

They researched and tested, and interviewed
Reconstructing some events in stages.
Explanations however remain elusive dreams
And controversies continue down the ages.

John Debenham

Historical Note: *Parts of Borley Parish Church date from the 12th century.*
The estate belonged to Barking Abbey until given by Henry VIII to Sir Edward Waldegrave at the dissolution of the monasteries. There are numerous ghostly legends and myths some dating from these times. The Rev. Henry Bull built Borley Rectory in 1863 and his descendants figure significantly in its history.
Modern interest dates from 1928 when the incumbent, Rev. Smith, asked the Daily Mirror for help. This resulted in a sensational article being published. The paper asked Harry Price, a member of the 'Society for Psychical research,' to investigate unexplainable happenings. The Rev. Lionel Foyster took over the living from 1930-35 when some of the strangest incidents occurred. In 1935 the house was sold. Price rented it and with his team conducted extensive research, much publicised in his two books 'The Most Haunted house in England' and 'The End of Borley Rectory.' In 1939 the house suffered a major fire allegedly caused by an overturned lamp. The ruins have since been demolished and modern housing now covers the site.

Happy Harry

Grey clouds, cold winds and rain give way to warmer days.
It's time to catch the train and head towards the sea.
Steam has given way to modern trains powered by electricity,
And the air is cleaner now.

The constant stop, start, and rattle of wheels over tracks of iron
Remind him of the countless journeys along this route over the years.
Journeys to the same spot in the same road, in the same town.

Along the prom, past the penny arcades,
where the seekers of thrills spend their pennies hoping for a miracle.
He stands still and looks around.
Yes, the Candy Floss stall is still there,
But the half-crown boat trip to the end of the pier has gone.

Wind ripples, pages flutter, children laugh,
Black and white specks in the sky screech in a cacophony of sound,
as he starts to read aloud:
'Please stop, please listen, I bring you hope.'
They walk on by.
Read on, sing your song, speak from the heart.

Faces blur and reform as sinners pause in their perambulations.
People stop and listen in their hopes of something new.
Stories of faith and hope he tells,
Songs of joy he sings in his favourite key.
Coins are tossed to him, he bends to pick a few.
The yobos laugh as he drops them from his burning hand.

The crowds come and go, as the morning turns to evening.
It's time to go, but let us sing once more:
'I'm H. A. P. P. Y. I'm H. A. P. P. Y., I'm H. A. P.,
I'm H. A. P. I'm H. A. P. P. Y.

John F. Barr

***Historical Note:** Happy Harry's real name was Rev. George Wood. He preached from a soapbox on Southend's Seafront at a spot near the Kursaal starting in 1910. He was insulted frequently, occasionally kicked and beaten and had glasses, bricks and stones thrown at him. As the result of one incident he lost the sight of one eye. Failing health forced him to give up preaching in 1966 and he died in Streatham, London in 1974 aged 86. A plaque stands on a wall now, where he used to preach*

Two Sisters: Two Churches

Beornia and Synnove, two noble sisters full of spite,
Daughters of Rheda and Aeschere the noble Knight.
From birth they wanted everything they touched.
Each fighting for anything the other one clutched.

Despite Willinggale's serenity and their tender age
Arguments over simple things sent them into a rage.
Constantly bickering and always misbehaved,
Their father's favour they desperately craved.

Wily feminine charms they began to learn
As maturity and womanhood took their turn.
Tristram, Hasculf of Rhyddol's son became their prey
Both wanted him and plotted each to have their way.

Beornia was flirting with Tristram one day at dusk.
Synnove spying this grew mad with jealousy and lust.
Quarrelling before their father, a strict but righteous man,
Both accused poor Tristram of hatching a wicked plan.

Aeschere confronted Tristram enraged with what he'd heard,
Heated exchanges gave way to battle, Tristram drew his sword,
Mortally wounded Aeschere fell, struck by a blow to the head.
Tristram, from a deep stab wound, by morning too was dead.

The sisters overcome with grief each of them aghast
Differences forgotten in their loss, but it wouldn't last,
Vowing to do penance at the church on bended knee,
For evermore until the day of judgement set them free.

The truce arranged was short lived they could not be content,
Their acts of penitence in church changed to bitter argument.
The congregation demanded the feuding in church must cease.
The second church was built, now each could pray in peace.

Essex Man

Based on the story: Two Sisters Two Churches

Historical Note: *The story of the two churches on the same site in Willingale built by rival sisters is no more than that. The tale has been handed down for over 100 years. However the churches were built more that 200 years apart! Hervey D'Espania built the church of Willingale Spain after the Norman Conquest. The Second Church of Willingale Doe was built around 1320 by the D'Ou Family. At that time the local wool industry was growing, with consequent population increase, thus the first church was insufficient to accommodate the worshippers. Rather than pull it down and build a larger one, the D'Ou family built a second church on the site of the already consecrated land which meant a minimum of disruption. A new parish was created which gave the village a second priest. Since 1929 the two churches have been united. Willingale Spain, fell into disuse and became a virtual ruin. It was restored in the 1950s by the Friends of Friendless Churches. Today both churches fall within the parish of Willingale with Shellow and Berners Roding.*

'History is Bunk'

'History is Bunk', so Henry Ford said,
It means nothing we don't want tradition.
What matters today, you can take it as read,
Is what we make of our own volition.

Ford's 'Black Model T' was a great success
Built in Manchester, Ford was doing all right.
But the need to expand was plain to see
So they searched nation-wide for a suitable site.

Dagenham was perfect, a small town set to grow.
With good access by river, road and rail.
Pleased with the plans Henry said let's go
And inspect. He and Clara then promptly set sail.

As Mr and Mrs Robinson they chose to travel
Meeting political leaders, Royalty as well.
So impressed was Henry he signed his approval
His Dagenham built cars would soon start to sell.

While his views on 'BUNK' remain a mystery
The seed planted in Dagenham came to fruition.
It grew to play a part in Essex history
And the town became famous for its Ford tradition.

The models of cars Ford produced since then
Achieved both notoriety and fame.
Model 'T' to Mondeo, some long forgotten,
Have made ESSEX MAN, worthy of the name.

John Debenham

Historical note: *Ford USA, built the Model 'T' in Manchester from 1913. 'Mr and Mrs Robinson' came to England in 1928. In 1929 Ford Motor Co Ltd was formed and production at Dagenham began in 1931. In the 1950s the factory employed over 40,000 workers. Car production ceased in 2002. Dagenham is now Ford's world centre of excellence for diesel engine design and manufacture.*

Ford
AM13

FORD
KEV910

PLOTLANDERS

From London to Dunton they came, a trickle then a rush
Seeking respite from the overcrowded, noisy, smoky city crush.
They came to stake their claim to farms gone to seed.
Times were hard, soil poor, and there were mouths to feed.

So whole families wanting a weekend retreat or holiday home
Came to the countryside where it was clean and free to roam.
The available land was divided into small lots
And for only Ten Pounds you could buy two plots.

The Land Company hoped to make a killing
Using techniques worthy of time-share billing.
Many were caught, believing their tales,
Carried away in the 'Champagne Sales.'
Some maybe went beyond their means
To finally own the plot of their dreams.

Travelling from London at the weekend,
Tools in hand and chores to attend.
The land having none of the normal utilities
They had confidence in their natural abilities.

Desirable plots were near Laindon Station
But dwellings sprang up in every location
Tents, shacks, if they kept out the rain,
Even the carriages of an old railway train.
Proper huts and chalets later would come
And for many these were 'home from home.'

In the 50s Londoners, descended again
On Basildon. Coming by car, bus or train
To new homes being built in a new town
On land that the 'plotlanders' used to own.
These former residents selling out one by one
Brought an end to an era whose time was gone.

Andrew Summers

Historical Note: *The Plotands came about as a result of agricultural decline in the 1870s. Bankrupt farming land was divided into small plots and for five pounds it was possible to purchase a 'plot' measuring 20x150 feet. Sales peaked during the 1920s and 1930s. After World War II, with the desperate need to re-house many Londoners, Basildon New Town was created which resulted in the takeover over of most of the plotland sites.*

Where is Zlin?

The thirties brought depression across the land
Times were hard with no employment to hand
People flocked to Tilbury on hearing the news
Thomas Bata needed people to make his shoes.

"Looking for a job boy?" enquired the booming voice
"Yes," I meekly answered. I hadn't any choice.
To be offered a job was most satisfactory
I thought, following Mr Schmidt into the factory.

Two days later I got my card to 'clock on'
Just in time, as most of my savings were gone.
The bosses didn't speak the English language
Which put us all at a great disadvantage.

I was sent to Czechoslovakia on a training course
One of only ten from the whole workforce.
Travelling by ferry from Harwich to 'The Hook',
Then by train. Twenty-four hours it took.

Arriving in Moravia at a town called Zlin,
This was where my training would begin.
I worked and studied for weeks in this situation
With trainees and workers from many a nation

My course completed, new skills, new learning.
We returned back to England, ambition burning.
In Tilbury leather plant my career began anew
Applying the techniques I'd been trained into.

Andrew Summers

Historical Note: *Thomas Bata, was to shoes what Ford was to motor cars. A Czechoslovakian national, he died in a plane crash in 1932. His son, Thomas junior, continued his work. The East Tilbury Bata Estate reflected the company ethos of 'A well housed, healthy workforce was a productive one'. It was built on former farmland in 1933, providing housing, restaurants, a ballroom, a cinema, a social club and even a daily newspaper. Each factory gate had a clock and a tannoy system played rousing marching music to the arriving and departing workers. Bata were good employers but absenteeism and lateness were not tolerated. Most of Bata East Tilbury closed in the 1980s with mainstream production transferred overseas.*

THE LITTLE SHIPS OF LEIGH - MAY 1940

Defender, Endeavour, Letitia
Reliant, Renown and Resolute :-

Were the little ships sent from Leigh
They had to join 800 more
To sail to Dunkirk's distant shore
And change a course of history.

The convoy sailed past Margate pier
Their course set firm and true
The treacherous Channel surf died down
As if to help the bawleys through.

A shallow slope led to the beach
Not unlike the one at Leigh
But this one was under fire
From the Wehrmacht enemy.

300,000 men were trapped
And so the gallant fleet
Moved in to lift them from the sands
Out to a deeper reach.

The Renown was blasted by a mine
And all her crew men died
A memorial stone stands by Leigh Church
To tell their names with pride.

*'Greater love hath no man than this
That a man lay down his life for his friends.'*

Shirley Baker

Historical note: *Winston Churchill, described the Dunkirk evacuation as a "miracle of deliverance". 'Operation Dynamo' as it was called lasted 10 days. Apart from shipping the RAF lost 177 aircraft over Dunkirk. The historic old wooden cockle boat 'Endeavour' has returned to Leigh following major renovation work.*

Striking back

After the dark days of forty one,
There was a job that needed to be done.
No longer just defending the land
Taking the fight to the enemy was planned.

In Spitfires, Mosquitoes, Bostons painted black
Canadians and Belgians, and Brits braved the flack.
From Bradwell-on-Sea the pathfinders went
To mark the targets, then bombers were sent.

Squadrons of fighter wings were formed
To support the troops when beaches were stormed.
More and more aircraft flew to escort
Paratroopers to Arnhem for battles to be fought.

Lastly from here rescue planes would race
To find aircrews ditched when returning to base.
But a brave 121 who left Bradwell Bay;
They never came back to this very day.

Andrew Summers

***Historical Note:** RAF Bradwell Bay became operational in April 1942 with the arrival of a Canadian Squadron. Over the next three years over 20 squadrons operated from this airfield involved in a whole variety of support missions. Bradwell Bay was closed in December 1945. The site was then developed as Britain's first Nuclear Power Station. A memorial to the crews lost or missing stands on the corner of the original site.*

Mulberry
Here we go round

Trips around the Mulberry
And tales of yester year
That sailor men have told to me
Whilst holding back a tear –
Of days of yore before the mast
When summer sails were set for Kent,
Of ship ahoy, the lubber's last,
Before the tide was spent.

Of music on the afterdeck
And dancing in the sun,
Of stories spun around wrecks,
Of smugglers and rum –
Of mutiny and merry yarns,
Of piracy and storms,
Of tars a-top the tallest arms,
Of lobster pots and prawns.

Trips around the Mulberry
And memories abaft
That sailor men have told to me
When slanting on the past –
Of tack and turn or ride the road,
Of gybe and haul the sheet,
Of sky aloft and sea below,
Of run and yaw and beat.

Of all aboard the beams of light
That bounce across the briny brow,
Of gulls astern and horses white
And voices in the shrouds –
Of barge and barque and brigantine,
Of bawley, ketch and yawl,
Of every craft the coast has seen
In weathers fair or squall.

Trips around the Mulberry
And gunwales washed with foam,
Of waves awash the listing lee
And spray that's ever blown –
Of days of yore before the mast
When summer sails were set for Kent,
Of ship ahoy, the lubber's last,
Before the tide was spent.

Mervyn Linford

Historical Note: *A 'Phoenix' caisson, its back broken, lies on The West Knock sandbank just over a mile (1.8 km off Thorpe Bay). The caisson was a section of the temporary 'Mulberry Harbour' intended to be used in the Normandy landings following D Day. This section was being towed from Immingham, to Southsea. It sprang a leak and was brought into the Thames Estuary and allowed to sink. Other than being used as a code name there was no significance in the word Mulberry.*

Down the River Lea

In the 9th century the river Lea
Once formed a natural boundary
Between the Viking invaders domain
And where the Saxon Kings did reign.

Legend has it that when the Danes
Sailed up the river and landed,
King Alfred and a few of his Thanes
Blocked its flow and left them stranded.

Later mills making gunpowder and flour
Used the River's constant waterpower.
Down stream by boat the produce went
To be put in stores in Essex and in Kent.

Industry thrived on the banks of the Lea
With transport via the Thames out to sea
Prospering here outside the Capitals core,
Slaughterhouses, soap, gasworks and more.

From the manufacturing of small arms,
To toys and fruit from covered farms.
Edmonton and Ponders End the base
For new technologies growing apace.

Electronics, plastics, telecommunications,
Heavy industry too. In transportation
Buses and railway locomotives were built
And ironclad ships in the rivermouth's silt.

London's population grew ever outward
And the cry for land by industry was heard.
One by one the old factories moved away
Housing, parks and shopping came to stay.

River conservation was the new watchword
Fishing and boating were the topics preferred.
Soon an Olympic village will start to take place
To impress the world with Lea valley's new face.

Essex Man

Historical Note: *The River Lea rises at Leagrave Marsh in Luton, Bedfordshire and is 52 miles (83kms) in length from its source to its junction with the Thames at Bow. It is possible to walk the whole length of the river. The river Lea formed London's border with Essex until local government reorganisation in London 1965. With London the host of the Olympic Games in 2012 the Lea Valley is about to be transformed.*

ARMAGEDDON

Into the bowels of the earth
Went the six hundred, the chosen few.
Into the modern day ARK,
A concrete bunker with blast doors new.

Who were the six hundred so entombed?
A cross section of society perhaps.
Or important people to ensure life goes on
When the destruction of all else has passed.

Seventy-five feet down they were buried
With food, water and three months support.
They would be able to broadcast to the world.
But would anyone be out there to report?

"We've left behind a green and pleasant land.
And if Armageddon comes, what we dread
Is that there's nobody left up there to be found.
Are we, the chosen few, the living dead?"

Armageddon never came
It was all a game of bluff.
Both sides played the game
Till both had had enough.

John Debenham

Historical note: *RGHQ51.1 Kelvedon Hatch, Essex. Nuclear Bunker. Built in great secrecy it was ready for occupation in 1952. This Regional Government Centre was to be activated in the event of a nuclear war. It was decommissioned in 1992 and is now open to the public as a tourist attraction. The 600 essential personnel; leaders, politicians, military, police, planners, engineers and doctors amongst others, were chosen to monitor the conflict and reconstruct a post war society. Happily they were not called upon.*

The Great Surge

The weather for Friday was forecast to be cold
Off Iceland a deep depression had gained hold.
Moving south-easterly this low created
Gales that for two days never abated.

Pushing tons of Atlantic water south
Swelling every North Sea river's mouth
Building on top of a high spring tide
A wall of water that had no place to hide.

On Saturday morning all was normal on the Essex shore
Wind and tides were high, but this had happened before.
Events went ahead as planned, a dance on Clacton Pier,
A memorial on Canvey Island- what was there to fear?

The first bad news, a Ferry had sunk at Stranraer in the bay
132 had drowned. But the Irish Sea? That was far away.
Night came, the surge increased as further south it travelled
Reaching Essex and one by one the sea defences unravelled.

By midnight, Harwich and Maldon were flooded,
Over sea walls at Jaywick the water thudded.
Around midnight Canvey's barriers came down
And the sea, uninvited, swept through the town.

Up the Thames the great surge still raced unchecked
What stood in its path, it overwhelmed and wrecked.
Dawn revealed death and destruction, all seemed lost.
With daylight came rescue and time to reckon the cost.

Art Szmauz

Historical note: *The great storm surge of 31st January 1953 broke through 1200 sea defence sites. 32,000 thousand people had to be evacuated. 113 deaths were recorded in Essex, including 58 at Canvey Island and 37 in Jaywick. In Jaywick 7000 were made homeless and for a time the whole of Canvey Island was evacuated. (The devastation to the coast of The Netherlands was also disastrous) Considerable efforts have since been made to strengthen coastal defences including new sea walls at Canvey and Jaywick, and the showpiece Thames Barrier.*

Magnox

On the banks of the Blackwater, the old Magnox stands
Encased in concrete on the edge of the Dengie lands.
This grey monster was Britain's first, the oldest of its type,
Now pensioned off, though born with considerable hype.

Deep within a protective shield a chain reaction was made
By smashing uranium atoms with neutrons in a great fusillade.
This created heat, then steam which turned the turbines
Making electricity to send along the national grid lines.

For forty years Bradwell station supplied the necessary power
From Southend, to Colchester including the Layer Marney Tower.
The technology was welcomed in the fifties, though still untried,
But many were the difficulties and costs continually multiplied.

Waste disposal was the problem, so the end was near
In 2002 power generation ceased at Easter that year.
Outside the gates, the enthusiasts stood quietly and cried.
Others shouted 'good riddance' on the day the old beast died.

Andrew Summers

Historical Note: Built on the site of old Bradwell Bay airfield, Britain's first Nuclear Power station began to generate commercial quantities of electricity in 1962. Magnox is short for magnesium non-oxidising, but the design soon became obsolete. Bradwell stopped generating electricity in 2002 as it was no longer economic to operate. It is estimated 10 years will be needed to decommission and defuel the plant. It is not yet known when the site could be used for other purposes.

Writing on the Wall

If you ever come to Walden by the single track,
You're advised to place your luggage firmly in the rack,
And walk the two odd miles at a steady easy pace,
For it will prove the quickest way of getting to the place.

There have been tales, perhaps untrue, of our own local train,
When, all the travellers getting in and out again,
Still found themselves at Audley End, the driver very kind,
Had brought the engine home – and left the carriages behind!

CM
Courtesy of Walden Weekly News 1949

Historical Note: *The closure of the Audley End - Saffron Walden Branch line was an early victim of the Beeching cuts which shut over 4000 miles of rail line between 1964 and 1974. The last train from Saffron Walden was the 8.09pm Sunday Night service in September 1964. Although the above poem was written some 15 years before the Saffron Branch line closed it was clear its days were numbered even then.*

PIRATE ASHORE

In January 66, a vicious snow laden wind hit the ship,
The mooring stretched, strained and began to rip.
As conditions deteriorated the vessel broke free,
And was tossed around in the boiling sea.

Mi Amigo's transmitters sent an SOS
"Help! Come quickly we're in distress."
Walton lifeboat launched to save the crew
But was helpless as the sea's fury grew.

Then on to Frinton's beach the ship came crashing,
Driven onshore by the mighty storms lashing.
Cables were laid from ship to shore
And a breeches buoy rescued the beleaguered four.

The weather had succeeded, where government had failed,
To silence the transmitter when the pirates first sailed.
For Radio Caroline the weather was only a setback
For within a few weeks it was back on track.

Andrew Summers

Historical Note:** 'Radio Caroline', the first offshore 'pirate' station aimed at a UK audience started broadcasting on March 29 1964. DJ Simon Dee uttered the following words:* ***"Hello everybody. This is Radio Caroline, broadcasting on 199, your all-day music station."
The station took its name from Caroline Kennedy, daughter of the late U.S. President John F. Kennedy. The 1967 Marine Offences Act closed most of the Pirate stations. Six weeks after the act became law the BBC introduced its national pop station Radio 1. The 'Mi Amigo', converted from a small cargo boat, was built in 1921 in Germany with the name 'SS Margarethe'.

Essex Boys

It was 2 to 1 up with seconds to go.
Then as tension built came a terrible blow.
Germany scored and snatched the match back.
The England team was now on the rack.

With extra time now needed to settle the game,
Captain Bobby Moore called each player by name.
The manager stepped forward into the throng.
The players wondering how it had gone wrong.

Ramsay eyeing his men spoke calmly and plain.
"All right. You let it slip. Now start again." [1]
They listened in silence as he spoke.
He wondered what reaction his words would provoke.

His team were inspired, a second goal from Hurst
Was followed by a third in a last seconds burst
As Ken Wolstenholme said, wiping his brow,
"Some of the crowd are on the pitch,
they think it's all over - It is now." [2]

Essex Man

Historical Note: *England won the World Cup on 30th July 1966 and lifted The Jules Rimet Trophy. They beat West Germany 4-2 after extra time. The talk by the Manager at the break between full time and extra time was inspirational in lifting the team's spirits. The England Team contained 3 Essex Boys, - the Manager, Alf Ramsay, from Dagenham, Booby Moore the Captain from Barking and Martin Peters from Plaistow. Geoff Hurst, who scored 3 goals in the final, was also considered an honorary Essex boy having spent his best playing years at West Ham. Alf Ramsay was knighted in 1970 but died in somewhat obscurity in 1999. The Captain on the day, Booby Moore, became manager of Southend United between 1984 and 1986 but sadly died of cancer in 1993.*

[1] *The words of Alf Ramsay*

[2] *The words of BBC Commentator at the match, Ken Wolstenholme*

Let It Rock!

1000s came on foot, or by bus, car, train or ferry
And it wasn't to Woodstock, Reading or Glastonbury
Anyone who was cool and hip came along
Plus Hippies and Angels, what could go wrong?

T. Rex, Rod Stewart and Status Quo topped the bill
With Mott the Hoople, and Mungo Jerry set to thrill.
From Friday to Bank Holiday Monday it was non stop rock
With dozens of bands playing around the clock.

It was just electric, amazing, and magical
Being August 1971 in its way quite radical.
Peace, love and understanding in Weeley
This event happened in Essex, oh really!

Andrew Summers

Historical Note: *Nearly 150,000 attended the Weeley Rock Festival. Dozens of bands performed. The Rock festival was planned by the Clacton Round Table as a charity event and as an alternative to the previous year's donkey derby. It had been hoped to get six local bands and perhaps 5 – 10 thousand spectators. During the festival a public address was made to find 'Wally' who had been separated from his friends. The call of 'Where's Wally' was taken up by the crowd with its consequent imprint on the language to this day.*

The Enterprise has Landed

It was Stansted's biggest crowd puller to date
And 200,000 visitors passed through the gate,
VIPs took their seats under skies blue and bright,
And news cameras rolled to capture the sight

'The Enterprise' was what they'd all come to see.
On the fifth of June nineteen-eighty-three
The shuttle arrived in style, piggyback,
On a Boeing 747 with a special roof rack.

Fitzhugh Fulton the pilot, of the US Airforce,
Brought his plane to a stop right on the concourse.
Shuttle and mother ship basked in the gaze
Of enthusiastic visitors for two further days.

A re-usable space vehicle, the first of its kind,
Bringing dreams of space travel for all to mind.
A DC3 with sightseers from Southend flew there
Giving birds-eye views of the shuttle from the air.

On the third day the jumbo with the shuttle on top
Bade farewell to Essex, flying on to the next stop.
Airport life soon returned to the summer norm
Of queues of holidaymakers flying to Benidorm.

Glenis Summers

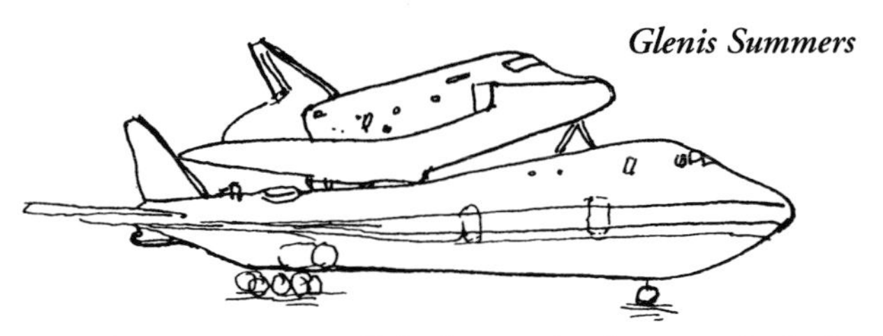

Historical note: *Stansted Airport was originally built as a USAF base in 1943. In the 1960s it was designated London's third airport. The new terminal was opened by the Queen in 1991. Stansted Airport's corporate address, Enterprise House was named in honour of the shuttle's visit. On site there is also a meeting room called the Fulton. The Enterprise never went into space but was used to test landing procedures. The first shuttle to fly in 'space' was the 'Colombia' in April 1981. This same craft disintegrated during re-entry on 1 February 2003 at the end of its 28th mission. All seven crew members aboard died.*

Lambs to the Slaughter

The first lorry came down the winding road.
A January evening chilled the load
What thoughts went through the driver's mind?
At narrow junctions, what would he find?

1,000 people faced him on that first night
Having been out since dawn exerting their right.
Eggs and nails flew, some tried to break the glass
Others lay in the road to impede the truck's pass.

On day two weather halted the bleating cargo.
Boats waited as gales enforced an embargo.
Next day riot police made extraordinary scenes
Clearing demonstrators by all available means.

By April the public order act was invoked
Protesters thought their liberties were revoked.
At the time it was still a legal export trade,
The police insisted the law must be obeyed.

Arrests and fines were the order of the day.
Then a protester died after having his say.
Injunctions were issued; which gave a blow
To police-community relations, already quite low.

Into autumn the daily confrontations occurred.
Then, "all shipments will cease," was the good news heard.
Police, lorries and protesters, all drifted away
And peace reigned once more at the dock on the bay.

Art Szmauz

Historical Note: *Live animal exports started in January 1995 from Brightlingsea and continued every day, weather permitting until Friday 27th October 1995. Nearly one million live animals were exported annually from the UK up to 2001. When Foot and Mouth disease broke out in February that year the trade in live animal export ceased. Restrictions were lifted in July 2002. Currently live animal exports are estimated at approximately 60,000 per annum, over 90% down on the pre 2001 figure.*

Windmills on my Mind

Windmills, Windmills, turning in the breeze,
Grinding corn to flour with ease.
White weatherboarded rotating tower,
Man in union with natural power.

Latticed sails spin round and round,
Pumping water from under ground,
Moving with a tranquil grace,
The ever shifting winds to face.

They strode the land in days gone by,
Now steel poles spring up standing high.
The same winds now turn an aerofoil;
Electricity no more comes from coal or oil.

From Dagenham's industrial heartland they creep,
Across Essex, to the sea. They never sleep,
They buzz and whirr, speaking to their own kind
But not to me, or the windmills on my mind.

Essex Man

Historical Note: *Although windmills have been around for more than 600 years in wasn't until 1830 that wind milling in Essex peaked. They were mainly used for pumping water and grinding flour. By 1950 most had ceased to be used commercially due to steam or electric driven alternatives. Those that survived were destined to become heritage attractions. However, with high fossil fuel prices and environmental concerns, windmills in the form of wind turbines were revived. In Dagenham, at the Ford plant, wind turbines are used as the main power source for assembling high-tech diesel engines. In the North Sea off Clacton the London Array project is underway. This has plans for a 341 turbine wind farm which when completed will be one of the largest in Europe.*

NOTES

AND FINALLY

This book has used poetry as a vehicle to illuminate people, events and places that have formed our history. Although we make no claim to literary merit as our primary intention is to be informative, we would claim to be following a poetic tradition long established in Essex.

In the 16th century *Thomas Tusser* of Rivenhall used poetry to great effect in his treatise on 'Good Husbandry'. *William Morris* of Walthamstow, better known for his arts and crafts movement but a poet nevertheless, was a 19th century contemporary of *Gerard Manley Hopkins* who was born in Stratford when that village was firmly in Essex. In the early 20th century *Ruth Pitter* was befriended by *Hillaire Belloc* and admired by *Yeats and C.S. Lewis.* She was born in Ilford as was her near contemporary *Denise Leventov. Leventov* was admired and encouraged by *TS Elliot.* She emigrated to America where she found wide acclaim.

Currently an Essex man is at the forefront of poetry in England. *Andrew Motion,* born and raised in Stisted near Braintree, is Poet Laureate. One of his predecessors in the post, *Alfred Lord Tennyson,* lived for a time at High Beach in Epping where he wrote 'In Memoriam'.

Poetically we could not, and should not, be included in such illustrious company. We have simply tried to show that our Essex heritage has much to offer and that poetry is an interesting way of exploring it.

If your interest has been aroused, the following pages provide a list of contacts and locations to enable further exploration of the history of this great county of Essex.

John Debenham

Locations and Contact Addresses

(By poetic subject)

Armageddon
Kelvedon Hatch Secret Nuclear Bunker
Kelvedon Hall Lane,
Great Myles Ongar Road,
Kelvedon Hatch CM14 5TZ
Tel: 01277 364 883
www.japar.demon.co.uk

Bertram the Clown
Clacton Pier
Tel: 01255 421115
www.clactonpier.co.uk

Boudica and Under Seige
Colchester Castle Museum, Castle Park,
Colchester CO1 1YG
Tel: 01206 282939.
www.colchestermuseums.org.uk
Tourist Information Centre Colchester
Tel: 01206 282290
e-mail: vic@colchester.gov.uk

Chapel on the Wall
The Chapel of St Peter-on-the-Wall
Bradwell-on-Sea, Essex.
Othona Community Enquiries,Tel: 0621 776564

Coalhouse Fort and It's Not Cricket
Coalhouse Fort, Princess Margaret Road
East Tilbury Village, Tilbury RM11 2AS
Tel: 01375 844203
www.coalhousefort.co.uk

Dear Diary
Audley End House and Gardens
Saffron Walden CB11 4JF
Tel: 01799 522399.
www.english-heritage.org.uk

Dissolution
Leez Priory, Hartford End,
Great Leighs, Chelmsford CM3 1JP
Tel: 01245 362 555
www.brideshead.co.uk/leez

Dunmow Flitch and Doctor's Pond
Great Dunmow Museum, Mill Lane,
Dunmow, Essex, CM6 1BG.
Tel: 01371 878979
www.greatdunmowmuseum.org.uk
Dunmow Community Information Office
Council Offices, Great Dunmow
Tel: 01799 510490

The Duke of Boulogne
Mountfitchet Castle,
Stansted Mountfitchet,
Essex CM24 8SP
Tel: 01279 813237
www.mountfitchetcastle.com

Dutch Cottage Museum,
Canvey Road, Canvey Island,
Tel: 01268 794005

Elected by 32
Harwich Guildhall, Church Street, Harwich
Tel: 01255 503429

Family Courtauld
Braintree District Museum
Manor St, Braintree, CM7 3HT
Tel: 01376 325266
www.enjoybraintreedistrict.co.uk/museum

Fairlop Frigate
Valence House Museum
Becontree Avenue
Dagenham
RM8 3HT
Tel: 020 8270 6865

Grave Diggers
Chelmsford Cathedral
New Street Chelmsford CM1 1TY
Tel: 01245 294480
www.chelmsfordcathedral.org.uk

Harbingers at Harlow
Museum of Harlow,
Muskham Road, (off First Avenue),
Harlow, Essex CM20 2LF
Tel: 01279 454959
www.harlow.gov.uk

History is Bunk
Ford Motor Works
Dagenham
www.ford.co.uk

John Constable's Schooldays
Constable Country
Bridge Cottage, Flatford, Dedham C07 60L
Tel: 01206 298260
www.nationaltrust.org.uk/flatford

Joscelyne's Beach
Adjacent to Chalkwell railway station
Southend-on-Sea.
(See bibliography – Joscelyne, Arthur.)

Just Mad about Saffron
Saffron Walden Museum, Museum Street,
Saffron Walden, Essex CB10 1JL
Tel: 01799 510333/4
Uttlesford Tourist and Community Information Centre
1 Market Place, Saffron Walden, Essex CB10 1HR
Tel: 01799 510444
www.uttlesford.gov.uk

Layer Marney Tower
Maldon Road, (Signposted from B1022)
Layer Marney, Colchester CO5 9US
Tel: 01206 330784
www.layermarneytower.co.uk

Little Ships to Dunkirk
The Endeavour Trust
Keith Threadgold, Secretary
44 Lansdowne Avenue,
Leigh-on-Sea SS9 1LL
Tel: 01702 713 325

Longer than a Mile
Southend Pier Museum
Southend Pier, Western Esplanade
Southend-on-Sea SS1 1EE
Tel: 01702 611214
www.southendpiermuseum.com

Magna Carta (de Vere's) and Dog of War
Hedingham Castle
Castle Hedingham, Essex. CO9 3DJ
Tel: 01787 460261
www.hedinghamcastle.co.uk

Magnox
Bradwell Nuclear Power Station
Bradwell-on-Sea,
Southminster CM0 7HP
Tel: 01621 776331
www.britishnucleargroup.com

Not a lot of people know that.
Tourist Information Centre Waltham Abbey
Highbridge Street, Waltham Abbey, EN9 1DG
Tel: 01992 652295
and also the Abbey
The Parish Office, 5a Greenyard,
Waltham Abbey, Essex, EN9 1RD.
Tel: 01992 767897
www.walthamabbeychurch.co.uk

Onward Christian Soldiers
St Edmunds Church, East Mersey,
Church Lane, Mersey Essex

Pirate Ashore
Radio Caroline,
The Maidstone Studios, Vinters Park,
Maidstone, Kent ME14 5NZ
Tel: 01622 684400
www.radiocaroline.co.uk

Plotlanders
Langdon Visitor's Centre
Third Avenue, Lower Dunton Road
Basildon SS16 6EB
Tel: 01268 419103
www.ukattraction.com/east-of-england/langdon-visitors-centre

Radio 2MT
Chelmsford Visitor Information Centre
Chelmsford Rail Station
Duke Street, Chelmsford CM1 1HT
Tel: 01245 283400
www.marconicalling.com

Sad Days at High Beech
Epping Forest Visitors Centre
Nursery Road, High Beach, Epping
Tel: 0208 8508 0028
www.cityoflondon.gov.uk

Salvation Army Colony
Salvation Army-Hadleigh Farm,
Castle Lane, Benfleet SS7 2AP
Tel: 01702 558550
www.hadleighfarm.co.uk

Sea Witch
Leigh Heritage Centre
13a High Street,
Leigh-On-Sea SS9 2EN
Tel: 01702 470834

Thames Barge
Topsail Charters
Cooks Barge Yard
The Hythe, Maldon CM9 5HN
Tel: 01621 857567

Thaxted
Thaxted Information Centre
7 Town Street, Thaxted CM6 2PJ
Tel: 01371 831641
www.thaxted.co.uk

Three Days that shook the Kingdom
Brentwood Tourist Information Centre
44 High St, Brentwood CM14 4AJ
Tel: 01277 200300

Three Mills at Battlesbridge
Battlesbridge Antiques Centre
Hawk Hill, Battlesbridge SS11 7RE
Tel: 01268 575000 / 764197
www.battlesbridge.com

Tiptree Jam
Wilkin & Sons Limited,
Tiptree CO5 0RF
Tel: 01621-814524 (Visitor centre)
www.tiptree.com

Walton Tower
Walton on the Naze
Tel: 07966776417
The Naze Protection Society,
Tel: 01255 676868
www.ukattraction.com/east-of-england/naze-tower

William Byrd
Stondon Place, Stondon Massey.
Also Ingatestone Hall,
Ingatestone. CM4 9NR
Tel: 01277 353010

William Morris
William Morris Gallery
Lloyd Park, Forest Road
London E17 4PP
Tel: 020 8527 3782
www.walthamforest.gov.uk/wmg/

For more general research.

Southend Poetry Group
meets at 8.00pm on the first Wednesday
of each month upstairs in the Railway Hotel,
Clifftown Road, Southend on Sea, Essex.
www.southendpoetry.co.uk

Essex County Council Libraries
(More than 70 in Essex)
PO Box 882, Market Road
Chelmsford CM1 1LH
Telephone: 01245 492758
www.essexcc.gov.uk/libraries

Essex Records Office
Wharf Road,
Chelmsford CM2 6YT
Tel: 01245 244644
www.essexcc.gov.uk/ero

Southend on Sea Libraries
Southend Central Library
Victoria Avenue
Southend SS2 6EX
Tel. 01702 534100
www.southend.gov.uk

Thurrock Libraries
Thameside Complex, Orsett Road,
Grays RM17 5DX
www.thurrock.gov.uk/libraries

Whilst every care has been taken to ensure the accuracy of the above information the editors are unable to accept responsibility for its content which has been supplied in good faith.

About the Authors

Shirley Baker

Shirley Baker lives in Leigh-on-Sea, Essex and has published poems on a wide variety of subjects. She is a member of the Southend Poetry Group. As a mature student she obtained a B.A. Honours degree in Art History and Literature. She has really enjoyed the challenge of researching her poems about Historical Essex.

John F Barr

John Barr was born in Essex and worked as a Chartered Surveyor until retiring in 2005. As a change from "bean counting" he attended a Poetry workshop run by Barbara Maskens in 1998. With Barbara's encouragement, his first shaky attempts were translated from thoughts to paper, leading to several poems being published in the Southend Poetry Group's anthologies over the last few years.

Christine Billington

Has been writing since a teenager. One of her poems won a bursary with the Arvon foundation. Since then Christine has had several collections of poetry published by K.T. Publications and many pieces taken by small press publishers.

Karen Bowman

Prize winner in a national poetry competition, enthusiastic author of published poems, short stories and of numerous factual and descriptive features for county magazines, Karen loves researching her subjects as much as writing them. Now working on a book of county interest for a national publisher. One of the newest members of the Southend Poetry Group she finds writing poems 'most therapeutic.'

John Debenham

Born in Romford John has always lived in Essex. On retirement from engineering he took a BA History degree followed by an MA in Intellectual History, studying 'civilisation and barbarism'. A member of Southend Poetry Society and Rocheway writing group he writes poetry and short stories with longer works in 'perpetual progress' and enjoys historical research.

Essex Man

The chosen pseudonym 'Essex Man' reflects a certain pride in all that the county has to offer. His poetry draws on a long experience of living within its borders and an interest in its history for most of his adult life. Contrary to outdated modern perceptions 'Essex Man' is always willing to listen to the views of others and adapt his work to fit in with the contemporary mood.

Robert Hallmann

As an apprentice in Germany Robert learned typesetting by hand (like Gutenberg). He has since worked in Holland, Wales, Hertfordshire, Dublin and London where, as a freelancer he has been involved in all aspects of publishing covering; advertising, typography, graphics, artwork and photography. As well as many magazine features and book illustrations his published work includes poetry, children's poems and prose. His books 'Benfleet – A History' was published in 2005 and 'Essex – History You Can See' and 'Canvey, a pictorial History' in 2006.

Clare Harvey

Born in Wiltshire, but of an old Leigh bloodline, Clare was educated in Leigh and Westcliff. She is a founder member of a Kidney Patients Association which raised £2m to establish a renal unit for Southend. Since retiring in 2001 from a career in training, education and the probation service, Clare concentrates on her 5 grandchildren, poetry, photography, painting, gardening, swimming and her long term partner – Mervyn!

Mervyn Linford

Mervyn Linford has been writing poetry for over thirty years. He has had work published in many magazines, periodicals and anthologies and has been broadcast on both local and national radio. He has had seven collections of poetry published and four works of prose. He runs the Littoral Press and is Poetry Editor for Pentacle Magazine. He was one of the readers at the Essex Poetry Festival in October 2004.

Katie Mallett

Katie Mallett has written poems and articles since the 1980s. She has contributed verse and prose to Essex magazines and newspapers, and for five and a half years was the BBC Essex Poet. She has won numerous competitions and her work has appeared in various anthologies, including a series of books edited by E.O. Parrott published by Penguin/Viking.

Adrian Green

Adrian Green lives overlooking the sea at Southend. He has degrees in psychology and general arts as well as a post-graduate diploma in humanities. He is a former editor of SOL magazine, reviews editor of Littoral, and has published 2 pamphlet collections - Beachgame and The Watchers. His poems and reviews have been published in a number of local and international magazines, anthologies and websites.

Margaret Rice

A love of language and literature has featured throughout Margaret's life. Originally from Northamptonshire, she moved to London where she raised a family, worked as a teacher and local government officer and sang, soprano, with the 'Crouch End Festival Chorus'. After retirement she gained a BA degree followed by an MA in History and Philosophy. Her writing focused particularly on poetry after moving to Essex in 2003 where, until her death in June 2006, she produced some of her most observant and poignant work.

Andrew Summers

Born within the sound of Bow Bells, Andrew has now lived for the last 18 years in Hadleigh. The Essex Hundred has proved quite a challenge. Previously the author of the quickly forgotten 'How to Get the Best from Your Printer' Andrew has perhaps uniquely worked for Britain's largest company and also Britain's smallest company. He has been married to Glenis for 40 years.

Art Szmauz

An immigrant to the county with established roots in Southend. He comes from a family of teachers, actors and musicians which he feels has given him a unique outlook and opportunity to study the subjects encountered in Essex from several conflicting points of view.

And the Artist: Elizabeth Summers

Elizabeth lives in Suffolk and is a member of the Sudbourne Park Printmakers Group. She has illustrated several books and is an accomplished printmaker and painter in oils. Her work is regularly exhibited locally and was featured prominently at Aldeburgh's Peter Pears Gallery Easter showing as well as the recent Art Expo in Antwerp in Belgium.

SELECTED BIBLIOGRAPHY

Addison, William. *Essex worthies : a biographical companion to the County.* Phillimore, 1973.

Basildon Branch Libraries. *Billericay and the New World: a summary.* Essex County Library, 1970.

Carter, Douglas, *Short History of Boxted,* 1996

Carter, M.H. *The fort of Othona and the Chapel of St Peter-on-the-Wall.* Provost and Chapter of Chelmsford, 1966.

Chelmsford Museum Service. *Guglielmo Marconi, 1874-1937 : the father of wireless.* Chelmsford Museum

Chisenhale-Marsh, T.C.(Trans.) *Domesday Book relating to Essex.* W.D. Burrell, 1864.

Clark, Dr Michael. *Rochford Hall : the history of a Tudor house and biographies of its owners.* Alan Sutton, 1990.

Colthorpe, M and Bateman, L.H. *Queen Elizabeth I and Harlow.* Harlow Development Corporation, 1997.

Currie, I. Davidson, M. Ogley, R.*The Essex Weather Book.* Froglets, 1992.

Dudley, Donald.R. *The rebellion of Boudicca.* Routledge and Kegan Paul, 1962.

Embleton, Paul: *Around Stansted Mountfitchet.* Tempus Publishing 1999

Essex Telegraph. *Full account of the calamitous earthquake in East Essex on Tuesday morning, April 22nd 1884 : reprinted from The Essex telegraph.* Frederic Wright, 1884

Essex Village Book Compiled by:Federation of Essex Womens Institutes. Countryside, 2001.

Grun, Bernard. *The Timetables of History.* Simon and Schuster, 1982.

Humphries, Ralph. C. *Radio Caroline : the pirate years.* Oakwood, c2003.

Jacobs, Norman. *Clacton on Sea: a Pictorial History.* Phillimore, 1993.

Joscelyne, Arthur. *Joscelyne's beach : a memoir of Leigh-on-Sea.* Desert Island, 2004.

Joscelyne, Arthur. *Joscelyne's tales of old Leigh and Chalkwell.* Desert Island, 2005.

Knights, E. Spurgeon. *William Byrd and Stondon Massey : a great musician and his life in Essex.* Essex Review, 1934.

Lake, Hazel. *The Arkwrights and Harlow.* (the author)1996.

SELECTED BIBLIOGRAPHY

Latham, R. and Matthews,W; Eds. *The Diary of Samuel Pepys.* Bell & Hyman, 1983.

Lemmon, David & Marshall, Mike, *Essex County Cricket Club,* Kingswood Press, 1987.

Lewis, Jim. *London's Lea Valley : Britain's best kept secret.* Phillimore, 1999.

Lockwood, Martin. *The Coggeshall Gang.* Essex Police Museum, 1995.

Male, Dr D. A. and Kemp-Luck Mrs A. *From Serf to Citizen,* Harwich Town Council, 2004.

Marriage, John. *Barging into Chelmsford : the story of the Chelmer and Blackwater navigation.* Ian Henry, 1997.

Morgan, Glyn. *Essex witches : the witches, enchantments, charms and sorcerers of Essex.* Spurbooks, 1973.

Morgan, Glyn. *Secret Essex.* Ian Henry, 1994.

Neale, Kenneth, *Essex 'full of profitable thinges'* Leopard's Head Press, 1996 .

O'Leary, J.G. *The Book of Dagenham.* Borough of Dagenham, 1964

Price, Harry. *The most haunted house in England : ten years' investigation of Borley Rectory* Chivers Press, 1975.

Rumble, Alexander. Ed. *Doomsday Book Essex.* Phillimore, 1983.

Scott, E.V. *The Best of Essex Countryside.* County guide Publications, 1976

Scott, Winifred N. *Coryton. History of a Village,* Mobil, 1981

Shepherd, E.W. *The Story of Southend Pier - and its associations.* Egon, 1979.

Sipple, Mavis. *Rochford A History,* Phillimore, 2004.

Smith, Michael. *I am just going outside : Captain Oates - Antarctic tragedy.* Spellmount, 2002.

Vingoe, Lesley. *Hockley, Hullbridge and Hawkwell Past.* Phillimore, 1999.

Webber, Ronald. *Peasants Revolt.* Terrance Dalton,1980.

Yearsley, Ian. *Essex events : death, disaster, war and weather.* Phillimore, 1999.

Yearsley, Ian. *Hadleigh Past.* Phillimore,1998.

Already available

The Essex Hundred

2000 years of Essex History.
100 Poems with historical notes, timelines and locations.
ISBN 978955229503
Paperback 164 pages.
RRP £7.99

The Essex Hundred Colouring Book

A local colouring book for children
with easy to follow historical notes
ISBN 9780955229527
Paperback 40 pages, size 297 X 210 RRP £3.99

and

The Essex Hundred Illustrated Map

ISBN 9780955229510
A3 map 297mm x 410mm
RRP £2.50 (includes VAT)

Coming soon

The New Essex Hundred

ISBN 9780955229541

and

The Essex Hundred Note Book

ISBN 9780955229558

All enquiries
e-mail: ask@essex100.com
www.essex100.com